UNDERSTANDING
HUMAN NATURE

THE AUTHOR'S PRINCIPAL WORKS:

Organ Inferiority and Its Physical Compensation

The Neurotic Constitution

The Practice and Theory of Individual Psychology

The Case of Miss R

Problems of Neurosis

The Case of Miss A

The Pattern of Life

UNDERSTANDING HUMAN NATURE

BY

ALFRED ADLER

TRANSLATED BY WALTER BÉRAN WOLFE, M.D.
INTRODUCTION BY LELAND E. HINSIE, M.D.

PERMABOOKS

14 WEST 49TH ST., NEW YORK

INTRODUCTION

Self understanding is the first law of happiness. It can be acquired today by the average individual in a way and to an extent that was not possible a half century ago. The prime requirement is a sincere wish to see oneself and others with as much objectivity as can be gained by everyday observations as well as by the literature coming from those who have made the study of human nature their professional life effort.

Alfred Adler was above all a human being, kind in his frankness, honest in his appraisal of those who sought his help, and sincere in spreading the truths as he saw them through his vast experiences. He had an insatiable urge to get people to think about themselves and others, because he knew that the better understanding emerging from an appreciation of the fountainheads of human nature gives man a sense of security that could not be as soundly inculcated in him by any other means.

Because he knew the deeply scientific nature of the subject to which he devoted his life, but particularly because he also clearly recognized how to solicit the interests of those to whom the terms psychiatry and psychology were formidable, he was excellently equipped to play a leading role in the dissemination of the major facts relating to the sources of human behavior. He knew that he could best serve his fellow man by emphasizing and reemphasizing the inferior role into which children are born and their efforts over the succeeding years to grow from the dependency of childhood to the independency of maturity.

Adler stressed the significance of parental and social influences upon the infancy and early childhood of the human being, showing as others, notably Freud, was then demonstrating, that the patterns of adult adjustment are to a great extent laid down in the earliest years of life. The child has not only his own biological drives with which to contend, but also those of his parents, his brothers and sisters, later his teachers. In the vast majority of instances, the manner by which the child's own impulses combine with those of the parents especially, determines to a large degree success or failure in adult situations. Adler develops this point of view with particular clarity for the general public to whom he addresses his remarks. He seemed to have had a fine appreciation of the kind of information that could most easily be grasped by those to whom this viewpoint was new. Prior to his time, human nature was conceived in the light of physical forces, of body activities. It was believed that the distortions of human nature had to wait for solution upon researches in the field of organic medicine. Adler and his contemporaries, reared in the science of the body, soon came to know by practical experiences that many of the ills of human beings were understandable and treatable in terms of the personal habit patterns based upon early interpersonal relationships.

Adler was a pupil of Freud and, like many pupils, he differed in his thinking and practice, yet he always stayed with the concept of emotional conflict as a decisive contributing element in mental deviations. His basic ideas are well illustrated in this book.

To those who are aggrieved by the manner of their living, to those who are looking for the general source of their discomfitures and for the means by which to gain relief, Adler's *Understanding Human Nature* is a promising guide.

LELAND E. HINSIE, M.D.
Professor of Psychiatry, College of Physicians and Surgeons, Columbia University.
Assistant Director, New York State Psychiatric Institute and Hospital.

CONTENTS

UNDERSTANDING
HUMAN NATURE

INTRODUCTION

"The destiny of man lies in his soul."

HERODOTUS

The science of human nature may not be approached with too much presumption and pride. On the contrary, its understanding stamps those who practice it with a certain modesty. The problem of human nature is one which presents an enormous task, whose solution has been the goal of our culture since time immemorial. It is a science that can not be pursued with the sole purpose of developing occasional experts. Only the understanding of human nature by every human being can be its proper goal. This is a sore point with academic investigators who consider their researches the exclusive property of a scientific group.

Owing to our isolated life none of us knows very much about human nature. In former times it was impossible for human beings to live such isolated lives as they live today. We have from the earliest days of our childhood few connections with humanity. The family isolates us. Our whole way of living inhibits that necessary intimate contact with our fellow men, which is essential for the development of the science and art of knowing human nature. Since we do not find sufficient contact with our fellow men, we become their enemies. Our behavior towards them is often mistaken, and our judgments frequently false, simply because we do not adequately understand human nature. It is an oft-repeated truism that human beings walk past, and talk past, each other, fail to make contacts, because they approach each other as strangers, not only in society, but also in the very narrow circle of the family. There is no more frequent complaint than the complaint of parents that they cannot understand their children, and that of children that they are misunderstood by their parents. Our whole attitude toward our fellow man is dependent upon our understanding of him; an implicit necessity for understanding him therefore is a fundamental of the social relationship. Human beings would live together more easily if their knowledge of human nature were more satisfactory. Disturbing social relationships could then be obviated, for we know that unfortunate adjustments are possible only when we do not understand one another and are therefore exposed to the danger of being deceived by superficial dissimulations.

It is now our purpose to explain why an attempt is made to approach the problem from the standpoint of the medical sciences, with the objective of laying the foundations of an exact science in this enormous field; and to determine what the premises of this science of human nature must be, what problems it must solve, and what results might be expected from it.

In the first place, psychiatry is already a science which demands a tremendous knowledge of human nature. The psychiatrist must obtain insight into the soul of the neurotic patient as quickly and as accurately as possible. In this particular field of medicine one can judge, treat, and prescribe effectively only when one is quite sure of what is going on in the soul of the patient. Superficiality has no place here. Error is followed quickly by punishment, and the correct understanding of the ailment is crowned by success in the treatment. In other words, a very effective test of our knowledge of human nature occurs. In ordinary life, an error in the judgment of another human being need not be followed by dramatic consequences, for these may occur so long after the mistake has been made that the connection is not obvious. Often we find ourselves astonished to see what great misfortunes follow decades after a misinterpretation of a fellow man. Such dismal occurrences teach us the necessity and duty of every man to acquire a working knowledge of human nature.

Our examinations of nervous diseases prove that the psychic anomalies, complexes, mistakes, which are found in nervous diseases are fundamentally not different in structure from the activity of normal individuals. The same elements, the same premises, the same movements, are under consideration. The sole difference is that in the nervous patient they appear more marked, and are more easily recognized. The advantage of this discovery is that we can learn from the abnormal cases, and sharpen our eye for the discovery of related movements and characteristics in the normal psychic life. It is solely a question of that training, ardor, and patience which are required by any profession.

The first great discovery was this: the most important determinants of the structure of the soul life are generated in the earliest days of childhood. In itself this was not such an audacious discovery; similar findings had been made by the great students of all times. The novelty lay in the fact that we were able to join the childhood experiences, impressions, and attitudes, so far as we were capable of determining them, with the later phenomena of the soul life, in one incontrovertible and continuous pattern. In this way we were able to compare the experiences and attitudes of the earliest childhood days with the experiences and attitudes of the mature individual later on in life; and in this connection the important discovery was made that the single manifestations of the psychic life must never be regarded as entities sufficient unto themselves. It was learned that we could gain an understanding of these single manifestations only when we considered them as partial aspects of an indivisible whole, and that these single manifestations could be valued only when we could determine their place in the general stream of activity, in the general behavior pattern —only when we could discover the individual's whole style of life, and make perfectly clear that the secret goal of his childhood attitude was identical with his attitude in maturity. In short, it was proven with astonishing clarity that, from the standpoint of psychic movements, no change had taken place. The outer form, the concretization, the verbalization of certain psychic phenomena might change, but the fundamentals, the goal, the dynamics, everything which directed the psychic life towards its final objective, remained constant. A mature patient who has an anxious character, whose mind is constantly filled with doubts and mistrust, whose every effort is directed toward isolating himself from society, shows the identical character traits and psychic movements in his third and fourth year of life, though in their childish simplicity they are more transparently interpreted. We made it a rule therefore to direct the greater part of our investigation to the childhood of all patients; and thus we developed the art of being able, often, to reveal characteristics of a mature person whose childhood we knew, before we were told of them. What we observe in him as an adult we consider the direct projection of that which he has experienced in childhood.

When we hear the most vivid recollections of a patient's childhood, and know how to interpret these recollections correctly, we can reconstruct with great accuracy the pattern of his present character. In doing this we make use of the fact that an individual can deviate from the behavior into which he has grown in childhood only with great difficulty. Very few individuals have ever been able to change the behavior pattern of their childhood, though in adult life they have found themselves in entirely different situations. A change of attitude in adult life need not necessarily signify a change of behavior pattern. The psychic life does not change its foundation; the individual retains the same line of activity both in childhood and in maturity, leading us to deduce that his goal in life is also unaltered. There is another reason for concentrating our attention upon childhood experiences if we wish to change the behavior pattern. It makes little difference whether we alter the countless experiences and impressions of an individual in maturity; what is necessary is to discover the fundamental behavior pattern of our patient. Once this is understood we can learn his essential character and the correct interpretation of his illness.

The examination of the soul life of the child thus became the fulcrum of our science, and a great many researches were dedicated to the study of the first years of life. There is so much material in this field which has never been touched nor probed that everyone is in a position to discover new and valuable data which would prove of immense use in the study of human nature.

A method of preventing bad character traits was simultaneously developed, since our studies do not exist for their own sake but for the benefit of mankind. Quite without previous thought, our researches led into the field of pedagogy, to which we have contributed for years. Pedagogy is a veritable treasure-trove for any one who wishes to experiment in it, and apply to it what he has found valuable in the study of human nature, because pedagogy, like the science of human nature, is not to be got out of books, but must be acquired in the practical school of life.

We must identify ourselves with every manifestation of the soul life, live ourselves into it, accompany human beings through their joys and their sorrows, in much the same way that a good painter paints into a portrait those characteristics which he has felt in the person of his subject. The science of human nature is to be thought of as an art which has many instruments at its disposal, an art closely related to all other arts, and useful to them. In literature and poetry, particularly, it is of exceptional import. Its first object must be to enlarge our knowledge of human beings, that is to say, it must enable us all to acquire the possibility of fashioning for ourselves a better and a riper psychic development.

One of our great difficulties is that we very frequently

find people extraordinarily sensitive on just the point of their understanding of human nature. There are very few human beings who do not consider themselves masters in this science even though they have had very few studies preparatory to their degree; and there are even fewer such who would not feel offended if one would demand that they put their knowledge of mankind to the test. Those who really wish to know human nature are only those who have experienced the worth and value of people through their own empathy, that is, through the fact that they also have lived through psychic crises, or have been able to fully recognize them in others.

From this circumstance arises the problem and the necessity of finding a precise tactic and strategy, and a technique in the application of our knowledge. For nothing is more hateful, and nothing will be met with a more critical glance, than that we should brusquely throw into the face of an individual the stark facts which we have discovered in the exploration of his soul. It might be well to advise anyone who does not want to be hated that he be careful in this very connection. An excellent way to acquire a bad reputation is carelessly to make use of facts gained through a knowledge of human nature, and misuse them, as for instance in the desire to show how much one knows or has guessed concerning the character of one's neighbor at a dinner. It is also dangerous to cite merely the basic truths of this science as finished products, for the edification of someone who does not understand the science as a whole. Even those who do understand the science would feel themselves insulted through such a procedure. We must repeat what we have already said: the science of human nature compels us to modesty. We may not announce the results of our experiments unnecessarily and hastily. This would be germane only to a little child who was anxious to parade himself and show off all the things that he can do. It is hardly to be considered as an appropriate action for an adult.

We should advise the knower of the human soul first to test himself. He should never cast the results of his experiments which he has won in the service of mankind, into the face of an unwilling victim. He would only be making fresh difficulties for a still-growing science, and actually defeat his purpose! We should then have to bear the onus of mistakes which had arisen from the unthinking enthusiasm of young explorers. It is better to remain careful and mindful of the fact that we must have a complete whole in view before we can draw any conclusions about its parts. Such conclusions, furthermore, should be published only when we are quite certain that they are to someone's advantage. One can accomplish a great deal of mischief in a bad way, or at an improper moment, a correct conclusion concerning character.

We must now, before going on with our considerations, meet a certain objection which has already suggested itself to many readers. The foregoing assertion, that the style of life of the individual remains unchanged, will be incomprehensible to many, because an individual has so many experiences in life which change his attitude toward it. We must remember that any experience may have many interpretations. We will find that there are no two people who will draw the same conclusion from a similar experience. This accounts for the fact that our experiences do not always make us any cleverer. One learns to avoid some difficulties, it is true, and acquires a philosophical attitude towards others, but the pattern along which one acts does not change as a result of this. We will see in the course of our further considerations that a human being always employs his experiences to the same end. Closer examination reveals that all his experiences must fit into his style of life, into the mosaic of his life's pattern. It is proverbial that we fashion our own experiences. Everyone determines how and what he will experience. In our daily life we observe people drawing whatever conclusions they desire from their experiences. There is the man who constantly makes a certain mistake. If you succeed in convincing him of his mistake, his reactions will be varied. He may conclude that, as a matter of fact, it was high time to avoid this mistake. This is a very rare conclusion. More probably he will object that he has been making this mistake so long that he is now no longer able to rid himself of the habit. Or he will blame his parents, or his education, for his mistake; he may complain that he has never had anyone who ever cared for him, or that he was very much petted, or that he was brutally treated, and excuse his error with an alibi. Whatever excuse he makes, he betrays one thing, and that is that he wishes to be excused of further responsibility. In this manner he has an apparent justification and avoids all criticism of himself. He himself is never to blame. The reason he has never accomplished what he desired to do is always someone else's fault. What such individuals overlook is the fact that they themselves have made very few efforts to obviate their mistakes. They are far more anxious to remain in error, blaming their bad education with a certain fervor, for their faults. This is an effective alibi so long as they wish to have it so. The many possible interpretations of an experience and the possibility of drawing various conclusions from any single one, enables us to understand why a person does not change his behavior pattern, but turns and twists and distorts his experiences until they fit it. The hardest thing for human beings to do is to know themselves and to change themselves.

Any one who is not a master in the theory and technique of the science of human nature would experience great difficulty in attempting to educate human beings to be better men. He would be operating entirely on the surface, and would be drawn into the error of believing that because the external aspect of things had changed, he had accomplished something significant. Practical cases show us how little such technique will change an individual, and how all the seeming changes are only apparent changes, valueless so long as the behavior pattern itself has not been modified.

The business of transforming a human being is not a simple process. It demands a certain optimism and patience, and above all the exclusion of all personal vanity, since the individual to be transformed is not in duty bound to be an object of another's vanity. The process of transformation, moreover, must be conducted in such a way that it seems justified for the one changed. We can easily understand that some one will refuse a dish which would otherwise be very tasty to him if it is not prepared and offered to him in an appropriate manner.

The science of human nature has yet another aspect which we may call its social aspect. Human beings would doubtless get along with each other better, and would approach each other more closely, were they able to understand one another better. Under such circumstances it would be impossible for them to disappoint and deceive each other. An enormous danger to society lies in this possibility of deception. This danger must be demonstrated to our fellow-workers, whom we are introducing to this study. They must be capable of making those upon whom they are practicing their science understand the value of the unknown and unconscious forces working within us; in order to help them they must be cognizant of all the veiled, distorted, disguised tricks and legerdemain, of human behavior. To this end we must learn the science of human nature and practice it consciously with its social purpose in view.

Who is best fitted to collect the material of this science, and to practice it? We have already noted that it is impossible to practice this science only theoretically. It is not enough simply to know all the rules and data. It is necessary to transmute our studies into practice, and correlate them so that our eyes will acquire a sharper and deeper view than has been previously possible. This is the real purpose of the theoretical side of the science of human nature. But we can make this science living only when we step out into life itself and test and utilize the theories which we have gained. There is an important reason for our question. In the course of our education we acquire too little knowledge of human nature—and much of what we learn is incorrect, because contemporary education is still unsuited to give us a valid knowledge of the human soul. Every child is left entirely to himself to evaluate his experiences properly, and to develop himself beyond his classroom work. There is no tradition for the acquisition of a true knowledge of the human soul. The science of human nature finds itself today in the condition that chemistry occupied in the days of alchemy.

We have found that those who have not been torn out of their social relationships by the complicated muddle of our educational system are best adapted to pursue these researches in human nature. We are dealing with men and women who are, in the last analysis, either optimists, or fighting pessimists who have not been driven to resignation by their pessimism. But contact with humanity, alone, is not enough. There must be experience as well. A real appreciation for human nature, in the face of our inadequate education today, will be gained only by one class of human beings. These are the contrite sinners, either those who have been in the whirlpool of psychic life, entangled in all its mistakes and errors, and saved themselves out of it, or those who have been close to it and felt its currents touching them. Others naturally can learn it, especially when they have the gift of identification, the gift of empathy. The best knower of the human soul will be the one who has lived through passions himself. The contrite sinner seems as valuable a type in our day and age as he was in the days when the great religions developed. He stands much higher than a thousand righteous ones. How does this happen? An individual who has lifted himself above the difficulties of life, extricated himself from the swamp of living, found power to profit by bad experiences, and elevate himself as a result of them, understands the good and the bad sides of life. No one can compare with him in this understanding, certainly not the righteous one.

When we find an individual whose behavior pattern has rendered him incapable of a happy life, there arises out of our knowledge of human nature the implicit duty to aid him in readjusting the false perspectives with which he wanders through his life. We must give him better perspectives, perspectives which are adapted to the community, which are more appropriate for the achievement of happiness in this existence. We must give him a new system of thought, indicate another pattern for him in which the social feeling and the communal consciousness play a more important rôle. We do not purpose to make an ideal structure of his psychic life. A new viewpoint in itself is of great value to the perplexed, since from this he learns where he has gone astray in making his mistakes. According to our view the strict determinists who consider all human activity as the sequence of cause and effect are not far from wrong. Causality becomes a different causality, and the results of experience acquire entirely new values, when the power of self-knowledge and self-criticism is still alive, and remains a living motif. The ability to know one's self becomes greater when one can determine the wellsprings of his activity and the dynamics of his soul. Once he has understood this, he has become a different man and can no longer escape the inevitable consequences of his knowledge.

BOOK I

HUMAN BEHAVIOR

"Liberty alone breeds giants. Compulsion only kills and destroys."

II. The Function of the Psychic Organ

If we regard the function of the psychic organ from this standpoint, we will become aware that we are considering the evolution of a hereditary capability, an organ for offense and defense with which the living organism responds according to the situation in which it finds itself. The psychic life is a complex of aggressive and security-finding activities whose final purpose is to guarantee the continued existence on this earth of the human organism, and to enable him to securely accomplish his development. If we grant this premise, then further considerations grow out of it, which we deem necessary for a true conception of the soul. *We cannot imagine a psychic life which is isolated.* We can only imagine a psychic life bound up with its environment, which receives stimuli from the outside and somehow answers them, which disposes of capabilities and powers which are not fitted to secure the organism against the ravages of the outer world, or somehow bind it to these forces, in order to guarantee its life.

The relationships which suggest themselves from this are many. They had to do with the organism itself, the peculiarities of human beings, their physical nature, their assets and their defects. These are entirely relative concepts, since it is entirely a relative matter whether a power or an organ shall be interpreted as asset or liability. These values can be given only by the situations in which the individual finds himself. It is very well-known that the foot of man is, in a sense, a degenerate hand. In an animal which had to climb this would be of decided disadvantage, but for a man, who must walk on the flat ground, it is of such advantage that no one would prefer a "normal" hand to a "degenerate"

CHAPTER I

THE SOUL

I. The Concept and Premise of the Psychic Life

We attribute a soul only to moving, living organisms. The soul stands in innate relationship to free motion. Those organisms which are strongly rooted have no necessity for a soul. How supernatural it would be to attribute emotions and thoughts to a deeply rooted plant! To hold that a plant could, perhaps, accept pain which it could in no way escape, or that it could have a presentiment of that which it could not later avoid! To attribute reason and free will to it at the same time that we considered it a foregone conclusion that the plant could not make any use of its will! Under such conditions the will and the reason of the plant would of necessity remain sterile.

There is a strict corollary between movement and psychic life. This constitutes the difference between plant and animal. In the evolution of the psychic life, therefore, we must consider everything which is connected with movement. All the difficulties that are connected with change of place demand of the soul that it foresee, gather experiences, develop a memory, in order that the organism be better fitted for the business of life. We can ascertain then in the very beginning that the development of the psychic life is connected with movement, and that the evolution and progress of all those things which are accomplished by the soul are conditioned by the free movability of the organism. This movability stimulates, promotes, and requires an always greater intensification of the psychic life. Imagine an individual to whom we have predicated every movement, and we can conceive of his psychic life as at a standstill.

foot. As a matter of fact, in our personal lives, as in the lives of all peoples, inferiorities are not to be considered as the source of all evil. Only the situation can determine whether they are assets or liabilities. When we recall how variegated the relationships are between the cosmos, with its day and night, its dominance of the sun, its movability of atoms, and the psychic life of man, we realize how much these influences affect our psychic life.

III. Purposiveness (Teleology) in the Psychic Life

The first thing we can discover in the psychic trends is that the movements are directed toward a goal. We cannot, therefore, imagine the human soul as a sort of static whole. We can imagine it only as a complex of moving powers which are, however, the result of a unit cause, and which strive for the consummation of a single goal. This teleology, this striving for a goal, is innate in the concept of adaptation. We can only imagine a psychic life with a goal towards which the movements which exist in the psychic life, are directed.

The psychic life of man is determined by his goal. No human being can think, feel, will, dream, without all these activities being determined, continued, modified and directed, toward an ever-present objective. This results, of itself, from the necessity of the organism to adapt itself and respond to the environment. The bodily and psychic phenomena of human life are based upon those fundamentals which we have demonstrated. We cannot conceive of a psychic evolution except within the pattern of an ever-present objective, which is determined in itself by the dynamics of life. The goal itself we may conceive as changing or as static.

On this basis all phenomena of the soul life may be conceived as preparations for some future situation. It

seems hardly possible to recognize in the psychic organ, the soul, anything but a force acting toward a goal, and Individual Psychology considers all the manifestations of the human soul as though they were directed toward a goal.

Knowing the goal of an individual, and knowing, also, something of the world, we must understand what the movements and expressions of his life mean, and what their value is as a preparation for his goal. We must know also what type of movements this individual must make to reach his goal, just as we know what path a stone must take if we let it drop to earth, although the soul knows no natural law for the ever-present goal is always in flux. If, however, or has an ever-present goal, then every psychic tendency mu follow with a certain compulsion, as though there were a natural law which it obeyed. A law governing the psychic life exists, to be sure; but it is a man-made law. If anyone feels that the evidence is sufficient to warrant speaking of a psychic law he has been deceived by appearances, for when he believes that he has demonstrated the unchangeable nature and determination of circumstance, he has stacked the cards. If a painter desires to paint a picture, one attributes to him all the attitudes which are germane to an individual who has that goal before his eyes. He will make all the necessary movements with inevitable consequence, just as though there were a natural law at work. But is he under any necessity to paint the picture?

There is a difference between movements in nature and those in the human soul life. All the questions about free will hinge upon this important point. Nowadays it is believed that human will is not free. It is true that human will becomes bound as soon as it entangles itself or binds itself to a certain goal. And since circumstances in the cosmic, animal, and social relationships of man frequently determine this goal, it is not strange that the psychic life should often appear to us as though it were under the regency of unchangeable laws. But if a man, for example, denies his

relationships to society and fights them, or refuses to adapt himself to the facts of life, then all these seeming laws are abrogated and a new law steps in which is determined by the new goal. In the same manner, the law of communal life does not bind an individual who has become perplexed at life and attempts to extirpate his feeling for his fellowmen. And so we must assert that a movement in the psychic life must arise *of necessity* only when an appropriate goal has been posited.

On the other hand, it is quite possible to deduce what the goal of an individual must be from his present activities. This is of the greater importance because so few people know exactly what their goal is. In actual practice it is the procedure which we must follow in order to gain a knowledge of mankind. Since movements may have many meanings this is not always so simple. We can however take many movements of an individual, compare them, and graphically represent them; in this way we arrive at an understanding of a human being by connecting two points wherein a definite attitude of the psychic life was expressed, in which the difference in time is noted by a curve. This mechanism is utilized to obtain a unified impression of a whole life. An example will serve to illustrate how we may rediscover a childhood pattern in an adult, in all its astonishing similarity.

A certain thirty-year-old man of extraordinarily aggressive character, who achieved success and honor despite difficulties in his development, comes to the physician in circumstances of greatest depression, and complains that he has no desire to work or to live. He explains that he is about to be engaged, but that he looks at the future with great mistrust. He is plagued by a strong jealousy, and there is great danger that his engagement will be broken. The facts in the case, which he brings up to prove his point, are not very convincing. Since no one can reproach the young lady, the obvious distrust which he shows lays him open to suspicion. He is one of those many men who approach another individual, feel themselves attracted, but immediately assume an aggressive attitude, which destroys the very contact which they seek to establish.

Now let us plot the graph of this man's style of life as we have indicated above, by taking out one event in his life and seeking to join it up with his present attitude. According to our experience, we usually demand the first childhood remembrance, even though we know that it is not always possible to test the value of this remembrance objectively. This was his first childhood remembrance: he was at the market place with his mother and his younger brother. Because of the turmoil and crowding, his mother took him, the elder brother, on her arm. As she noticed her error, she put him down again and took the younger child up, leaving our patient to run around crushed by the crowd, very much perplexed. At that time he was four years old. In the recital of this remembrance, we hear the identical notes that we surmised in a description of his present complaint. He is not certain of being the favored one, and he cannot bear to think that another might be favored. Once the connection is made clear to him, our patient, very much astonished, sees the relationship immediately.

The goal toward which every human being's actions are directed, is determined by those influences and those impressions which the environment gives to the child. The ideal state, that is, the goal, of each human being, is probably formed in the first months of his life. Even at this time certain sensations play a rôle which evoke a response of joy or discomfort in the child. Here the first traces of a philosophy of life come to the surface, although expressed in the most primitive fashion. The fundamental factors which influence the soul life are fixed at the time when the child is still an infant. Upon these foundations a superstructure is built, which may be modified, influenced, transformed. A multiplicity of influences soon forces the child into a definite attitude towards life, and conditions his particular type of response to the problems which life gives.

Investigators who believe the characteristics of an adult are noticeable in his infancy are not far wrong; this accounts for the fact that character is often considered hereditary. But the concept that character and personality are inherited from one's parents is universally harmful because it hinders the educator in his task and cramps his confidence. The real reason for assuming that character is inherited lies elsewhere. This evasion enables anyone who has the task of education to escape his responsibilities by the simple gesture of blaming heredity for the pupil's failures. This, of course, is quite contrary to the purpose of education.

Our civilization makes important contributions to the determination of the goal. It sets boundaries against which a child batters himself until he finds a way to the fulfillment of his wishes which promises both security and adaptation to life. How much security the child demands in relation to the actualities of our culture may be learned early in his life. By security we do not consider only security from danger; we refer to that further coefficient of safety which guarantees the continued existence of the human organism under optimum circumstances, in very much the same way that we speak of the "coefficient of safety" in the operation of a well-planned machine. A child acquires this coefficient of safety by demanding a "plus" factor of safety greater than is necessary merely for the satisfaction of his given instincts, greater than would be necessary for a quiet development. Thus arises a new movement in his soul life. This new movement is, very plainly, a tendency toward domination and superiority. Like the grownup, a child wants to out-distance all his rivals. He strains for a superiority which will vouchsafe him that security and adaptation which are synonymous with the goal he has previously set for himself. There thus wells up a certain unrest in his psychic life which becomes markedly accentuated as time goes on. Suppose now that the world requires a more intensive response. If in this time of need the child does not believe in his own ability to overcome his difficulties we will notice his strenuous evasions and complicated alibis, which serve only to make the underlying thirst for glory the more evident.

In these circumstances the immediate goal frequently becomes the evasion of all greater difficulties. This type recoils from difficulties or wriggles out of them in order temporarily to evade the demands of life. We must understand that the reactions of the human soul are not final and absolute: every response is but a partial response, valid temporarily, but in no way to be considered a final solution of a problem. In the development of the child-soul especially, are we reminded that we are dealing with temporary crystallizations of the goal idea. We cannot apply the same criteria to the child soul that we use to measure the adult psyche. In the case of the child we must look farther and question the objective to which the energies and activities working themselves out in his life, would eventually lead him. Could we translate ourselves into his soul, we could understand how each expression of his power was appropriate to the ideal which he had created for himself as the crystallization of a final adaptation to life. We must assume the child's point of view if we want to know why he acts as he does. The feeling-tone connected with his point of view directs the child in various ways. There is the way of optimism, in which the child is confident of easily solving the problems which he meets. Under these circumstances he will grow up with the characteristics of an individual who considers the tasks of life eminently within his power. In his case we see the development of courage, openness, frankness, responsibility, industry, and the like. The opposite of this is the development of pessimism. Imagine the goal of the child who is not confident of being able to solve his problems! How dismal the world must appear to such a child! Here we find timidity, introspectiveness, distrust, and all those other characteristics and traits with which the weakling seeks to defend himself. His goal will lie beyond the boundaries of the attainable, but far behind the fighting front of life.

CHAPTER II

AL ASPECTS OF THE PSYCHIC LIFE

der to know how a man thinks, we have to examine
tionship to his fellowmen. The relation of man to
determined on the one hand by the very nature of
os, and is thus subject to change. On the other
determined by fixed institutions such as political
traditions in the community or nation. We cannot compre-
hend the psychic activities without at the same time understanding these social relationships.

I. The Absolute Truth

Man's soul cannot act as a free agent because the necessity of solving the problems which constantly arise, determines the line of its activity. These problems are indivisibly
bound up with the logic of man's communal life; the essential conditions of this group-existence influence the individual, yet the facts of the communal life seldom allow
themselves to be influenced by the individual, and then
only to a certain degree. The existing conditions of our
communal life however cannot yet be considered final; they
are too numerous, and are subject to much change and
transformation. We are hardly in a position to completely
illuminate the dark recesses of the problem of the psychic
life, and understand it thoroughly, since we can not escape
from the meshes of our own relationships.

Our sole recourse in this quandary is to assume the logic
of our group life as it exists on this planet as though it were

an ultimate absolute truth which we could app
by step after the conquest of mistakes and err
from our incomplete organization and our limite
ties as human beings.

An important aspect of our considerations l
materialistic stratification of society which Marx a
have described. According to their teaching, the
basis, the technical form in which a people lives, d
the "ideal, logical superstructure," the thinking and
of individuals. Our conception of the "logic of hum
munal life," of the "absolute truth," is in part an ag
with those concepts. History, and our insight into
the individual (that is, our Individual Psycholog
taught us however that it is occasionally expedient for the
individual to make a mistaken response to the demands of
an economic situation. In attempting to evade the economic
situation, he may become inextricably entangled in the
meshes of his own mistaken reactions. Our way to the absolute truth will lead over countless errors of this kind.

II. The Need for Communal Life

The rules of communal life are really just as self-explan-
atory as the laws of climate, which compel certain measures
for the protection against cold, for the building of houses,
and the like. The compulsion toward the community and
communal life exists in institutions whose forms we need
not entirely understand, as in religion, where the sanctifica-
tion of communal formulae serves as a bond between members of the community. If the conditions of our life are
determined in the first place by cosmic influences, they are
also further conditioned by the social and communal life
of human beings, and by the laws and regulations which
arise spontaneously from the communal life. The communal
need regulates all relationships between men. The com-

munal life of man antedates the individual life of man. In the history of human civilization no form of life whose foundations were not laid communally can be found. No human being ever appeared except in a community of human beings. This is very easily explained. The whole animal kingdom demonstrates the fundamental law that species whose members are incapable of facing the battle for self-preservation, gather new strength through herd life.

The herd instinct has served humanity to this end: the most notable instrument which it has developed against the rigors of the environment is the soul, whose very essence is permeated with the necessity of communal life. Darwin long ago drew attention to the fact that one never found weak animals living alone; we are forced to consider man among these weak animals, because he likewise is not strong enough to live alone. He can offer only little resistance to nature. He must supplement his feeble body with many artificial machines in order to continue his existence upon this planet. Imagine a man alone, and without an instrument of culture, in a primitive forest! He would be more inadequate than any other living organism. He has not the speed nor the power of other animals. He has not the teeth of the carnivore, nor the sense of hearing, nor the sharp eyes, which are necessary in the battle for existence. Man needs an extensive apparatus to guarantee his existence. His nutrition, his characteristics, and his style of life, demand an intensive program of protection.

Now we can understand why a human being can maintain his existence only when he has placed himself under particularly favorable conditions. These favorable conditions have been offered him by the social life. Social life became a necessity, because through the community and the division of labor in which every individual subordinated himself to the group, the species was enabled to continue its existence. Division of labor (which means essentially, civilization) alone is capable of making available to mankind those instruments of offense and defense which are responsible for all its possessions. Only after he learned the division of labor did man learn how to assert himself. Consider the difficulties of childbirth and the extraordinary precautions which are necessary for keeping a child alive during its first days! This care and precaution could be exercised only where there was such a division of labor. Think of the number of sicknesses and infirmities to which the human flesh is heir, particularly in its infancy, and you have some conception of the unusual amount of care which human life demands, some comprehension of the necessity of a social life! The community is the best guarantee of the continued existence of human beings!

III. Security and Adaptation

From the previous expositions we conclude that man, seen from the standpoint of nature, is an inferior organism. This feeling of his inferiority and insecurity is constantly present in his consciousness. It acts as an ever-present stimulus to the discovery of a better way and a finer technique in adapting himself to nature. This stimulus forces him to seek situations in which the disadvantages of the human status in the scheme of life will be obviated and minimized. At this point arises the necessity for a psychic organ which can effect the processes of adaptation and security. It would have been much harder to have made an organism out of the primitive and original man-animal, which would be capable of fighting nature to a standstill, by the addition of anatomic defenses such as horns, claws, or teeth. The psychic organ alone could render first-aid quickly, and compensate for the organic deficiencies of man. The very stimulation growing from an uninterrupted feeling of inadequacy, developed foresight and precaution in man, and caused his soul to develop to its present state, an organ of thinking, feeling, and acting. Since society has played an essential rôle in the process of adaptation, the psychic organ must reckon from the very beginning with the conditions of communal life. All its faculties are developed upon an identic basis: the logic of communal life.

In the origin of logic with its innate necessity for universal applicability we should doubtless find the next step in the development of man's soul. Only that which is universally useful is logical. Another instrument of the communal life is to be found in articulate speech, that miracle which distinguishes man from all other animals. The phenomenon of speech, whose forms clearly indicate its social origins, cannot be divorced from this same concept of universal usefulness. Speech would be absolutely unnecessary to an individual organism living alone. Speech is justified only in a community; it is a product of communal life, a bond between the individuals of the community. Proof for the correctness of this assumption is to be found in those individuals who have grown up under circumstances which have made contact with other human beings difficult or impossible. Some of these individuals have often evaded all connections with society for personal reasons, others are the victims of circumstance. In each case, they suffer from speech defects or difficulties and never acquire the talent for learning foreign languages. It is as though this bond can be fashioned and retained only when the contact with humanity is secure.

Speech has an enormously important value in the development of the human soul. Logical thinking is possible only with the premise of speech, which gives us the possibility of building up concepts and of understanding differences in values; the fashioning of concepts is not a private matter, but concerns all society. Our very thoughts and emotions are conceivable only when we premise their universal utility; our joy in the beautiful is based on the fact that the recognition, understanding, and feeling for the beautiful are universal. It follows that thoughts and concepts, like reason, understanding, logic, ethics, and æsthetics, have their origin in the social life of man; they are at the same time bonds between individuals whose purpose is to prevent the disintegration of civilization.

Desire and will may also be understood as aspects of man's situation as an individual. Will is but a tendency in the service of the feeling of inadequacy, an instrument for the attainment of the feeling of a satisfactory adaptation. To "will" means to feel this tendency, and to enter into its movement. Every voluntary act begins with a feeling of inadequacy, whose resolution proceeds toward a condition of satisfaction, of repose, and totality.

IV. The Social Feeling[1]

We may now understand that any rules that serve to secure the existence of mankind, such as legal codes, totem and taboo, superstition, or education, must be governed by the concept of the community and be appropriate to it. We have already examined this idea in the case of religion, and we find adaptation to the community is the most important function of the psychic organ, in the case of the individual, as in the case of society. What we call justice and righteousness, and consider most valuable in the human character, is essentially nothing more than the fulfillment of the conditions which arise in the social needs of man—

[1]Translator's Note—The word "Gemeinschaftsgefühl" for which no adequate English equivalent exists, has been rendered as "social feeling" throughout the book. "Gemeinschaftsgefühl" however connotes the sense of human solidarity, the connectedness of man to man in a cosmic relationship. Wherever the brief phrase "social feeling" has been used therefore, the wider connotation of a "sense of fellowship in the human community" should be borne in mind.

kind. These conditions give shape to the soul and direct its activity; responsibility, loyalty, frankness, love of truth, and the like are virtues which have been set up and retained only by the universally valid principle of communal life. We can judge a character as bad or good only from the standpoint of society. Character, just as any achievement in science, politics or art, becomes noteworthy only when it has proven its universal value. The criteria by which we can measure an individual are determined by his value to mankind in general. We compare an individual with the ideal picture of a fellowman, a man who overcomes the tasks and difficulties which lie before him, in a way which is useful to society in general, a man who has developed his social feeling to a high degree. According to the expression of Furtmüller, he is one "who plays the game of life according to the laws of society." In the course of our demonstrations it will become increasingly evident that no adequate man can grow up without cultivating a deep sense of his fellowship in humanity and practicing the art of being a human being.

CHAPTER III

CHILD AND SOCIETY

Society exacts certain obligations of us which influence the norms and forms of our life, as well as the development of our mind. Society has an organic basis. The point of tangency between the individual and society may be found in the fact of man's bisexuality. Not in the isolation of man and woman, but in the community of man and wife, does he satisfy the impulse of life and achieve security and guarantee his happiness. When we observe the slow development of a child, we may be certain no evolution of human life is possible without the presence of a protecting community. The various obligations of life carry in themselves the necessity for a division of labor which not only does not separate human beings, but strengthens their bonds.

Everyone must help his neighbor. Everyone must feel himself bound to his fellow man. The vital relationships of man to man have originated thus. We must now discuss in more detail some of these relationships which greet a child upon his birth.

I. The Situation of the Infant

Every child, dependent as he is on the help of the community, finds himself face to face with a world that gives and takes, that expects adaptation and satisfies life. His instincts are baffled in their fulfillment by obstacles whose conquest gives him pain. He realizes at an early age that there are other human beings who are able to satisfy their urges more completely, and are better prepared to live. His soul is born, one might say, in those situations of childhood which demand an organ of integration, whose function is to make a normal life possible. This the soul accomplishes by evaluating each situation and directing the organism to the next one, with the maximum satisfaction of instincts and the least possible friction. In this way he learns to over-value the size and stature which enable one to open a door, or the ability to move heavy objects, or the right of others to give commands and claim obedience to them. A desire to grow, to become as strong or even stronger than all others, arises in his soul. To dominate those who are gathered about him becomes his chief purpose in life, since his elders, though they act as if he were inferior, are obligated to him because of his very weakness. Two possibilities of action lie open to him. On the one hand, to continue activities and methods which he realizes the adults use, and on the other hand to demonstrate his weakness, which is felt by these same adults as an inexorable demand for their help. We shall continually find this branching of psychic tendencies in children.

The formation of types begins at this early period. Whereas some children develop in the direction of the acquisition of power and the selection of a courageous technique which results in their recognition, others seem to speculate on their own weaknesses, and attempt to demonstrate it in the most varied forms. One need but recall the attitude, the expression, and the bearing of individual children, to find individuals who fit into one group or the other. Every type has a meaning only as we understand its relationship to the environment. Reflections of environment are usually to be found in the behavior of any child.

The basis of educability lies in the striving of the child to compensate for his weaknesses. A thousand talents and capabilities arise from the stimulus of inadequacy. Now the situations of individual children are extraordinarily different. In the one case we are dealing with an environment which is hostile to the child and which gives him the impression that the whole world is an enemy country. The incomplete perspectives of child thought-processes explain this impression. If his education does not forestall this fallacy, the soul of such a child may develop so that in later years he will act always *as if* the world really were an enemy country. His impression of hostility will become accentuated as soon as he meets with greater difficulties in life. This occurs frequently in the case of children with inferior organ-systems. Such children greet their environment with an attitude entirely different from those who come into the world with relatively normal organs. Organic inferiority can express itself in difficulties of motion, in inadequacies of single organs, or in weakened resistance of the entire organism, which results in frequent sickness.

Difficulties in facing the world are not necessarily caused only by deficiencies of the childish organism. The unreasonable demands made on a child by a foolish environment (or the unfortunate manner in which these demands are presented to him) are comparable to actual difficulties in the environment. A child who desires to adapt himself to his environment suddenly finds difficulties lying in his way, especially where he grows up in an environment which has itself lost its courage and is imbued with a pessimism only too quickly transferred to the child.

II. The Influence of Difficulties

In view of the obstacles which approach every child from countless angles, it is not to be wondered at that his response is not always adequate. His psychic habits have but a short time to develop, and the child finds himself under the necessity of orientating himself to the unchangeable conditions of actuality, while his technique of adjustment is still immature. Whenever we consider any number of mistaken responses to the environment we find ourselves dealing with constant developmental attempts on the part of the soul to make a correct response and to progress throughout life as in a continual experiment. The thing which we particularly see in the expression of the child's behavior pattern is the type of response which an adolescent gives in a definite situation, in the course of his maturation. His response attitude gives us an insight into his soul. We must at the same time take cognizance of the fact that the responses of any individual, just as those of society, are not to be judged according to a pattern.

The obstacles a child meets with in the development of his soul usually result in the stunting or distortion of his social feeling. They may be divided into those which arise out of defects in his physical environment; such as originate in abnormal relationships in his economic, social, racial, or family circumstances; and further, into those which arise out of defect in his bodily organs. Our civilization is a culture which is based upon the health and adequacy of fully-developed organs. Therefore, a child whose important organs suffer defects is at a disadvantage in solving the problems of life. Children who learn to walk late, or who have difficulties of any kind in locomotion, or those who learn to speak late, who are clumsy for a long time because the development of their cerebral activity takes longer than in the case of the usual child, belong in this class. We all know how such children are constantly bumping themselves, are clumsy and slow, and carry with them a burden of bodily and psychic sorrows. They are obviously not tenderly touched by a world which was not appropriately fashioned for them. Difficulties which arise out of some such inadequate development are many. Of course there is always the possibility that in the course of time a compensation is established automatically without a scar remaining, if the bitterness of the psychic need has not, in the meantime, developed in the child an attitude of despair which is felt in his later life; such a state of affairs may be complicated, in addition, by economic helplessness. It is easy to understand that the fixed laws of human society are but poorly comprehended by defectively equipped children. They look with suspicion and mistrust at the opportunities which they see developing around them, and have the tendency to isolate themselves and evade their tasks. They have a peculiarly sharp sense of life's hostility, and they unconsciously exaggerate it. Their interest in the bitterness of life is much greater than in its brighter side. For the most part, they overrate both, so that theirs is a lifelong attitude of belligerency. They demand that an extraordinary amount of attention be paid to them, and of course they think far more of themselves than of others. They conceive of the necessary obligations of life more as difficulties than as stimuli. Soon a gulf, which is continually widened because of their hostility to their fellows, builds itself between them and their environment. Now they approach every experience with an exaggerated cautiousness, removing themselves farther and farther from the truth and actuality with every contact, and succeed only in continually making fresh difficulties for themselves.

Similar difficulties may arise when the normal tenderness of parents toward their children is not manifested to a proper degree. Whenever this occurs serious consequences for the development of the child ensue. The child's attitude becomes so fixed that he cannot recognize love nor make the proper use of it, because his instincts for tenderness have never been developed. It will be difficult to mobilize a child who has grown up in a family where there has never been a proper development of the feeling of tenderness, to the expression of any kind of tenderness. His whole attitude in life will be a gesture of escape, an evasion of all love and all tenderness. The identical effect may be produced by un-

thinking parents, educators, or other adults, who teach
children that love and tenderness are improper, ridiculous,
or unmanly, by impressing some pernicious motto upon
them. It is not so seldom that we find that a child is taught
that tenderness is ridiculous. This is especially the case
among those children who have often been ridiculed. Such
children are veritably afraid of showing emotions or feelings because they feel their tendency to show love toward
others is ridiculous and unmanly. They fight against normal
tenderness as though it were an instrument to enslave or
degrade them. Thus boundaries to the love life may be set
in early childhood. After a brutal education in which all
tenderness is dammed up and repressed, a child withdraws
from the circle of his environment, and loses, little by little,
contacts which are of utmost importance to his soul. Sometimes a single person in the environment offers an opportunity of concord; when this happens the child joins himself
to his friend in a very deep relation. This accounts for the
individuals who grow up with social relationships directed
to but a single person, whose social tendencies can never be
stretched to include more than one other human being. The
example of the boy who felt himself neglected when he
noticed that his mother was tender only to his younger
brother, and therefore wandered up and down through life
trying to find the warmth and affection which he had missed
from earliest childhood, is a case in point, which demonstrates the difficulties such a person may find in life. It goes
without saying that the education of such individuals proceeds only under pressure.

Education accompanied by too much tenderness is as
pernicious as education which proceeds without it. A pampered child, as much as a hated one, labors under great
difficulties. Where it is instituted, a desire for tenderness
arises which grows beyond all boundaries; the result is that
a petted child binds himself to one or more persons and
refuses to allow himself to be detached. The value of tender-

ness becomes so accentuated by various mistaken experiences that the child concludes that his own love enforces certain implicit responsibilities on his grown-ups. This is easily accomplished: the child says to his parents, "Because I love you, you must do this or that." It is this type of social dogma which frequently grows up within the circle of the family. No sooner does the child recognize a tendency like this on the part of others than he increases his own tenderness in order to make them more dependent upon him. The flaming up of such tenderness to one particular person in the family must always be kept in mind. There is no doubt that the future of a child is influenced injuriously by such training. His life becomes involved in the struggle to hold the tenderness of others by fair means or foul. To accomplish this he dares to use every means which lies at hand; he may attempt the subjugation of his rival, a brother or sister, or occupy himself with tale-bearing against them. Such a child will actually incite his brothers to misdeeds in order that he may be able to sun himself in the love of his parents in relative glory and righteousness. He applies a definite social pressure to his parents in order to fix their attention on himself. To do this he will leave no stone unturned until he occupies the limelight and has achieved more importance than any one else. He is lazy, or bad, for the sole purpose of giving his parents the task of busying themselves more with him; he becomes a model child, because he considers the attention of others a sort of reward.

After the discussion of these mechanisms we may conclude that anything may become a means to an end, once the pattern of psychic activity is fixed. The child may develop himself in an evil direction, in order to arrive at his goal, or he may become a model child, with the same goal in view. One can often observe how one of several children seeks the limelight through particular unruliness while another, being shrewder, attains the same goal through particular virtue.

With the petted children we may also group those who have had every difficulty removed from their path, whose capabilities have been belittled in a friendly way. They have never had an opportunity to meet responsibilities. Such children have all been denied every opportunity to make those preparations which are so necessary for future life. They are not prepared to make contacts with anyone who is willing to join with them, and are certainly not capable of making contacts with others, who, as a result of difficulties and errors in their own childhood, throw obstacles in the way of human contacts. Such children are utterly unprepared for life, because they have never had an opportunity to practice the conquest of difficulties. As soon as they step out of the hothouse atmosphere of the tiny kingdom of their home, they suffer defeats almost of necessity, for the reason that they cannot find any human being willing to assume the duties and responsibilities which they expect at the hands of their petting educators, nor in the degree to which they are accustomed.

All the phenomena of this type have one thing in common: they tend to the greater or lesser isolation of the child. Children whose gastro-intestinal tracts are defective assume a special attitude towards nutrition, and as a result go through an entirely different developmental process from children who are normal in this respect. Children with defective organs have a peculiar style of life which may eventually drive them into isolation. There are other children who do not clearly understand their connection with the environment, and actually try to avoid it. They cannot find a comrade, hold themselves distinct from the games of their companions, and, either envious of their fellows, or, despising the play of children of the same age, busy themselves in a shut-in preoccupation with their own private games. Isolation also threatens children who grow up under the pressure of an education marked by great strictness. Life will not appear in a favorable light to them, because they are expecting bad impressions on every hand. Either they have the impression that they must be tolerant of all difficulties and take up their sorrows in a humble way, or they feel like champions, ready to take up the battle with the environment they have always found hostile. Such children feel that life and its tasks are inordinately difficult; it is not hard to understand how such a child will be busied for the most part with the defense of his personal boundary lines, lest he suffer some defeat of his personality. We may expect him constantly to retain before his eyes an unfriendly picture of the outer world. Burdened by an exaggerated cautiousness, he develops a tendency to evade all greater difficulties, rather than to lay himself open to the dangers of a possible defeat.

A further common characteristic of these pampered children, which is a sign of their inadequately developed social feeling, is the fact that they think more of themselves than of others. In this trait one sees clearly their whole development toward a pessimistic philosophy of the world. It is impossible for them to be happy unless they find a solution for their false behavior pattern.

III. Man as a Social Being

We have been at some length to show how we can understand the personality of the individual only when we see him in his context, and judge him in his particular situation in the world. By situation we mean his place in the cosmos, and his attitude toward his environment and the problems of life, such as the challenges of occupation, contact, and union with his fellow men, which are inherent in his being. In this way we have been able to determine that the impressions which storm in upon every individual from the earliest days of his infancy influence his attitude throughout his whole life. One can determine how a child stands in relation to life a few months after his birth. It is impossible to confuse the behavior of two infants after these months because they have already demonstrated a well-defined pattern which becomes the clearer as they develop. Variations from the pattern do not occur. The child's psychic activity becomes increasingly permeated by his social relationships. The first evidence of the inborn social feeling unfolds in his early search for tenderness, which leads him to seek the proximity of adults. The child's love life is always directed towards others, not, as Freud would say, upon his own body. According to the person, these erotic strivings vary in their intensity and manifestation. In children who are more than two years old these differences may be demonstrated in their speech. Only under the stress of the most severe psychopathological degeneration does the social feeling which has become firmly based in the soul of every child at this time, forsake him. This social feeling remains throughout life, changed, colored, circumscribed in some cases, enlarged and broadened in others until it touches not only the members of his own family, but also his clan, his nation, and finally, the whole of humanity. It is possible that it may extend beyond these boundaries and express itself towards animals, plants, lifeless objects, or finally towards the whole cosmos. An understanding of the necessity for dealing with man as a social being is the essential conclusion of our studies. Once we have grasped this, we have gained an important adjunct to the understanding of man's behavior.

CHAPTER IV

THE WORLD WE LIVE IN

I. The Structure of our Cosmos

Owing to the fact that every human being must make an adjustment to his environment, his psychic mechanism has the faculty of taking up impressions from the outer world. In addition, the psychic mechanism pursues a definite aim according to a definite interpretation of the world, and along the lines of an ideal behavior pattern which dates from early childhood. Although we cannot express this cosmic interpretation and this goal in a definite and exact term, we can nevertheless describe it as an ever present aura, and as always in contradistinction to the feeling of inadequacy. Psychic movements can occur only when they have an innate goal. The construction of a goal, as we know, premises the capacity for change, and a certain freedom of movement. The spiritual enrichment which results from freedom of movement is not to be undervalued. A child who raises himself from the ground for the first time comes into an entirely new world, and in that second he somehow senses a hostile atmosphere. In his first attempt at movement, and particularly in rising to his feet and learning to walk, he experiences various degrees of difficulty, which may either strengthen or destroy his hope for the future. Impressions which grown-ups might consider unimportant or commonplace, may have an enormous influence on the child's soul and entirely shape his impression of the world in which he lives. In this way children who have had difficulties in locomotion construct an ideal for themselves which is permeated with violent and hasty movements; we can discover this ideal by asking them what their favorite

games are, or what they would like to do when they are
grown. Usually such children answer that they desire to be
automobile drivers, locomotive engineers, or the like—thus
signifying clearly their desire to overcome every difficulty
which hinders their freedom of movement. The goal of their
life is to attain a point at which their feeling of inferiority
and their sense of handicap is entirely removed by perfect
freedom of motion. It is readily understood that such a sense
of handicap can originate easily in the soul of a child who
has developed slowly, or has encountered much sickness in
his life. Similarly, children who have come into the world
with defects in their eyes attempt to translate the entire
world into more intensive visual concepts. Children who
have auditory defects show an intense interest for certain
tones which seem to sound more pleasant to them; in short,
they become "musical."

Of all the organs with which a child attempts the conquest of the world the sense organs are the most important
in the determination of the essential relationships to the
world in which he lives. It is through the sense organs that
one constructs one's cosmic picture. Above all, it is the eye
which approaches the environment, it is the visual world
predominantly which forces itself upon the attention of
every human being and gives him the main data in his experiences. The visual picture of the world in which we live
has an incomparable significance in that it deals with un-
changing, lasting bases, in contrast to the other sense organs,
the ear, the nose, the tongue, and the skin, which are sensitive solely to temporary stimuli. There are, however, individuals in whom the ear is the predominant organ. Here a
psychic fund of information based more particularly upon
acoustic values is created. In this case the soul might be
said to have a predominantly auditory constellation. Less
frequently we find individuals in whom motor activity is
predominant. A predominance of interest for olfactory or
gustatory stimuli determines another type, and of these, the

first type, which is more sensitive to smell, is under a relative disadvantage in our civilization. Then there are a number of children in whom the musculature plays the leading rôle. This group comes into the world characterized with a greater restlessness, which forces them to constant movement in childhood, and to greater activity in maturity. Such individuals are interested only in such activities in which the functioning muscles play the chief rôle. They exhibit their activity even during sleep, as anyone can prove for himself by observing them restlessly tossing about in their beds. We must class those "fidgety" children whose restlessness is often considered a vice, in this category. In general we can say that a child who does not approach the world with heightened interest in some one organ or organ group, whether these be his sense organs or his locomotive apparatus, hardly exists. From the impressions which his more sensitive organ gathers from the world each child constructs a picture of the world in which he lives. We can therefore understand a human being only when we know with what sense organs or organ-systems he approaches the world, because all his relationships are colored by this fact; his actions and reactions gain their value from our knowledge of the influence which his organic defects have had upon the constellation of his cosmic picture in his childhood, and thus upon his later development.

II. Elements in the Development of the Cosmic Picture

The ever present goal which determines all our activity influences also the choice, intensity, and activity of those particular psychic faculties which serve to give shape and meaning to the cosmic picture. This explains the fact that each of us experiences a very specific segment of life, or of a particular event, or, indeed of the entire world in which we live. Each of us values only that which is appropriate to his goal. A real understanding of the behavior of any human being is impossible without a clear comprehension of the secret goal which he is pursuing; nor can we evaluate every aspect of his behavior until we know that his whole activity has been influenced by this goal.

A. PERCEPTION

The impressions and stimuli which arise in the outer world are transmitted by means of the sense organs to the brain, where certain traces of them may be retained. On these vestiges are built the world of imagination and the world of memory. But a perception is never to be compared with a photographic image because something of the peculiar and individual quality of the person who perceives is inextricably bound up with it. One does not perceive everything that one sees. No two human beings react in quite the same way to the identical picture; if we ask them what they have perceived they will give very diverse answers. A child perceives only that in his environment which fits into a behavior pattern previously determined by a variety of causes. The perceptions of children whose visual desire is especially well developed have a predominantly visual character. The majority of mankind is probably visual-minded. Others fill in the mosaic picture of the world which they have created for themselves with predominantly auditory perceptions. These perceptions need not be strictly identical with actuality. Everyone is capable of reconfiguring and rearranging his contacts with the outer world to fit his life pattern. The individuality and uniqueness of a human being consists in *what* he perceives and *how* he perceives. Perception is more than a simple physical phenomenon; it is a psychic function from which we may draw the most far going conclusions concerning the inner life.

B. MEMORY

The development of the soul is intimately related to the necessity for activity, upon the basis of the facts of perception. The soul is innately related to the motility of the human organism, and its activities are determined by the goal and purpose of this motility. It is necessary for man to collect and arrange his stimuli and relationships to the world in which he lives, and his soul, as an organ of adaptation, must develop all those faculties which play a rôle in his defense and are otherwise active in maintaining his existence.

It is clear now that the individual response of the soul to the problems of life leaves traces in the structure of the soul. The functions of memory and evaluation are dominated by the necessity for adaptation. Without memories it would be impossible to exercise any precaution for the future. We may deduce that all recollections have an unconscious purpose within themselves. They are not fortuitous phenomena, but speak clearly the language of encouragement or of warning. There are no indifferent or nonsensical recollections. One can evaluate a recollection only when one is certain about the goal and purpose which it subserves. It is not important to know *why* one remembers certain things and forgets others. We remember those events whose recollection is important for a specific psychic tendency, because these recollections further an important underlying movement. We forget likewise all those events which detract from the fulfillment of a plan. We find thus that memory, too, is subordinated to the business of purposive adaptation, and that every memory is dominated by the goal idea which directs the personality-as-a-whole. A lasting recollection, *even though it is a false one,* as is often the case in childhood, where memories are frequently surcharged with a one-sided prejudice, may be transposed out of the realm of the conscious, and appear as an attitude, or as an emotional tone, or even as a philosophic point of view, if this be necessary for the attainment of the desired goal.

C. IMAGINATION

Nowhere does the uniqueness of an individual show more clearly than in the products of his fantasy and of his imagination. By imagination we mean the reproduction of a perception without the presence of the object itself which gave rise to it. In other words imagination is reproduced perception:—another evidence of the creative faculty of the soul. The product of imagination is not only the repetition of a perception (which in itself is a product of the creative power of the soul), but is an entirely new and unique product built upon the basis of the perception, just as the perception was created on the basis of physical sensations.

Now there are fantasies which far exceed the customary imagination in sharpness of focus. Such visions are so sharply outlined that they have a value not of imaginary products, but influence the behavior of the individual as though the absent stimulating object were actually present. We speak of *hallucinations,* when fantasies appear as though they were the result of an actually present stimulus. The conditions for the appearance of hallucinations are in no wise different from those which determine fantastic day dreams. Every hallucination is an artistic creation of the soul, shaped and constellated according to the goals and purposes of the particular individual in which it appears. Let us make this clear with an example.

An intelligent young woman married against the advice of her parents. Her parents were so angry at her mismarriage that they broke off all relations with her. In the course of time the young woman became convinced that her par-

ents had not treated her well, but many attempts at reconciliation failed because of the pride and obstinacy of both
parties. As a result of her marriage this young woman, who
belonged to an honored and wealthy family, had fallen into
rather impoverished circumstances. Yet externally no one
could observe any signs of unhappiness in her connubial
relations. One could have been quite reconciled to the fact
that she had made a good adjustment were it not for the
appearance of a very peculiar phenomenon in her life.

This girl had grown up as the favorite child of her father.
So intimate had been their relationship that their present
breach was the more remarkable. The occasion of her
marriage, however, caused her father to treat her very badly,
and their rupture was very deep. Even when her child was
born, her parents could not be moved to visit their daughter
or to see the child; the young woman took the harsh treatment of her parents the more to heart, because, actuated by
a great ambition, she was touched to the quick by their
attitude toward her in a situation in which she might well
have been treated with consideration.

We must remember that the mood of this young woman
was completely dominated by her ambition. It is this character trait which gives us an insight into the reasons why the
breach with her parents affected her so deeply. Her mother
was a stern, righteous person who had many good qualities,
although she had treated her daughter with a heavy hand.
She knew how to submit to her husband, at least so far as
outer appearances were concerned, without really relin-
quishing her own rank. Indeed she drew attention to her
submission with a certain pride, and considered it an honor.
Now in this family there was also a son who was considered
a chip of the old block and the future heir of the family
name. The fact that he was considered somewhat more
valuable than our young woman served only to spur her
ambition. The difficulties and poverty which this young
woman, educated in a comparatively sheltered atmosphere

all her life, was experiencing in her marriage, now caused her to think constantly and with ever increasing displeasure about the mistreatment she had received at the hands of her parents.

One night before she had fallen asleep it happened that a door opened and the Virgin Mary stepped to her bed and said: "Because I love you so well, I must tell you that you will die in the middle of December. I do not want you to be unprepared."

The young woman was not frightened by this apparition, but she wakened her husband and told him everything. On the next day she went to the physician and told him about it. It was a hallucination. The young woman maintained that she had seen and heard everything quite clearly. At first glance this seems impossible, yet when we apply the key of our knowledge we can understand it quite well. Here is the situation: a young woman who is very ambitious, and, as the examination shows, has the tendency to dominate everyone else, breaks with her parents and finds herself in poverty. It is quite understandable that a human being, in an effort to conquer everything in the physical sphere in which he lives, should approach God and converse with Him. If the Virgin Mary had remained only an imaginary figure (as is the case in prayer) no one would have found anything particularly noteworthy in this occurrence, but this young woman needed stronger arguments.

The phenomenon loses all its mystery when we understand what tricks the soul is capable of producing. Is not every human being who dreams in a similar position? The difference really is only this: that this young woman can dream while she is awake. We must add, too, that her feeling of depression has placed her ambition under greater tension. Now we become aware of the fact that actually another mother is coming to her, indeed, that Mother who in popular conception is the greatest Mother of all. These two mothers must stand in certain contrast to one another.

The Mother of God appeared because her own mother did *not* come. The apparition is an accusation against her own mother and her insufficient love for her child.

The young woman is now trying to find some way of proving that her parents are wrong. The middle of December is not an insignificant time. It is that time of the year in which people are more apt to consider their deeper relationships, when most human beings approach each other with a greater warmth, give presents, and the like. It is at this time too that the possibility of reconciliation comes closer, so that we can understand that this particular time stands in a close relationship to the quandary in which the young woman finds herself.

The only strange thing in this hallucination seems to be that the friendly approach of this Mother of God is accompanied by the sad news of the young woman's approaching death. The fact that she told her husband of this vision with an almost happy tone of voice is also not without significance. This prophecy quickly spread beyond the narrow circle of her family and the physician had learned of it on the following day: and it was thus very simple to bring it about that her mother actually visited her.

A few days later the Virgin Mary appeared for the second time and spoke the same words. When the young woman was asked how her meeting with her own mother had turned out, she answered that her mother could not admit that she had done wrong. We see therefore the old theme cropping up again. Her desire to dominate her mother had not yet been fulfilled.

At this time it was attempted to make the parents understand what was actually going on in the life of their daughter, and as a result, a very satisfactory meeting between the young woman and her father obtained. A touching scene occurred, but the young woman was not yet satisfied, because she said there was something theatrical in her father's behavior. She complained that he had let her

wait too long! Even in triumph she could not rid herself
of the tendency to prove everyone else wrong and herself
to appear in the light of a triumphant victor.

Another example will show how the creative power of the
soul can produce either an illusion or a hallucination, as the
need arises. A man of excellent family who had never
amounted to anything because of a bad education, held an
unimportant clerkship. He had given up all hope of ever
amounting to anything. His hopelessness weighed heavily
upon him, and in addition his psychic tension was increased
by the reproaches of his friends. In these circumstances he
took to drink, which gave him at once a sweet forgetfulness,
and an excuse for his failure. After some time he was
brought to the hospital in delirium tremens. Delirium is
closely related to hallucination, and in the delirium of alco-
holic intoxication, small animals, such as mice, or insects,
or snakes, frequently appear. Other hallucinations which are
related to the patient's occupation may also occur.

Our patient came into the hands of physicians who were
strongly opposed to the use of alcohol. They put him
through a strict course of treatment and he was completely
freed of his alcoholism, left the hospital cured, and did not
touch alcohol for three years. At this time he returned to
the hospital with a new complaint. He stated that he constantly saw a leering, grinning man who watched him at his
work. He was now a day-laborer. Once when he was particularly angry because this man was laughing at him he
took his pick and threw it at him to see whether he was a
real man or only an apparition. The apparition dodged the
missile, but thereupon attacked him and beat him badly.

In this case we can no longer speak of a ghost because
the hallucination had very real fists. The explanation is not
hard to find. It was his *custom* to hallucinate, but he made
his *test* upon a real man. This shows us clearly that although
he had been freed of his desire to drink, he had in reality
sunk further since his discharge from the hospital. He had

lost his job, had been put out of his house, and now had to earn his living as a day-laborer, which he as well as his friends considered the lowest form of work. The psychic tension in which he had lived had not become less. Although he had been freed from alcohol he had actually become poorer by a consolation, despite the great advantage of this cure. He could do his first job with the help of drink, for when he was reproached too loudly at home for not accomplishing anything, the excuse that he was a drunkard seemed less shameful to him than his incapability of holding a job. After his cure he was again face to face with reality and in a situation which was in no wise less oppressive than his former one. Should he now fail he had nothing to console himself with and nothing to blame, not even alcohol.

In this situation of psychic peril the hallucinations reappear. He identifies himself with the previous situation and looks at the world *as if* he were still a drunkard, and says very clearly with this gesture, that he has ruined his whole life with his drinking and nothing can be done about it now. By being sick he hoped to be freed from his little honored, and therefore, for him, very unpleasant occupation as a ditch digger, without having to make a decision about it himself. The above-mentioned hallucination lasted for a long time until he finally was forced to the hospital again. Now he could console himself with the thought that he could have accomplished a great deal more had not the misfortune of drink ruined his life. This mechanism enabled him to maintain his personal evaluation at a high level. It was more important for him not to allow his personal evaluation to sink than it was for him to work. All his efforts were directed at maintaining the conviction that he might have accomplished great things had he not been visited by misfortune. This was the proof which maintained him in his power relationship and enabled him to feel that other men were not better than he but that an impassable obstacle lay in his way. The mood in which he attempted to find a consoling alibi produced the apparition of the leering man; the ghost was the savior of his self-esteem.

III. Fantasy

Fantasy is but another creative faculty of the soul. Traces of this activity may be found in the various phenomena which we have already described. Just as the projection of certain memories into the sharp focus of consciousness, or the erection of the bizarre superstructures of the imagination, fantasy and day-dreaming are to be considered part of the creative activity of the soul. The prevision and prejudgment which are an essential faculty in any mobile organism constitute an important factor in fantasy. Fantasy is bound up with the mobility of the human organism and is indeed nothing more than a method of prevision and prescience. The fantasies of children and grown-ups, sometimes called day-dreams, are always concerned with the future, the "castles in the air" are the goal of their activity, built up in fictional form as models for real activity. Examinations of childhood fantasies show clearly that the striving for power plays the predominant rôle. Children deal with the goal of their ambition in their day-dreams. Most of their fantasies begin with the words "when I am grown up," and the like. There are many adults who live as though they still had to grow up. The clear emphasis on the striving for power indicates to us again that the soul life can develop only when a certain goal has been set. In our civilization this goal is the goal of social recognition and significance. An individual never remains long at any neutral goal, for the communal life of mankind is accompanied by constant self-measurement which gives rise to the desire for superiority, and the hope of success in competition. The forms of prevision which are so evident in the fantasies of children are almost entirely situations in which the child's power is expressed.

We must not generalize here because it is impossible to lay down rules for the degree of fantasy or the extent of imagination. What we have said before is valid for a number of cases, but may not be applicable to some. Those children who approach life with belligerent eyes will develop their fantastic powers to greater lengths because their precaution is stimulated to a greater tension as a result of their attitude. Weak children for whom life is not always pleasant develop greater powers of fantasy, and have the tendency to occupy themselves particularly with this type of activity. At a certain stage in their development their ability to imagine may become a mechanism whereby the realities of life are evaded. Fantasy may be misused as a condemnation of reality. In such cases it becomes a kind of power-intoxication in an individual who raises himself above the meanness of living, by the fictional lever of his imagination.

The social feeling, together with the striving for power, also plays a great rôle in the fantasy life. In childhood fantasies, it is only seldom that power strivings appear without some application of this power to social ends. This trait we see clearly in those fantasies in which the content concerns itself with being a savior or a good knight, a victor over evil forces, devils, and the like. The fantasy that the child does not belong to his own family frequently occurs. Many children believe that they actually originated from a different family, and that some day their real father, some important personage, will come and fetch them. This happens most frequently where children with a deep feeling of inferiority, hounded by the deprivations they have suffered, are forced into the background, or become dissatisfied with the love and tenderness they receive in their family circle. Ideas of grandeur betray themselves in the external attitude of the child who acts as though he were already grown up. Sometimes one finds almost pathological expressions of this fantasy, as for instance, in children who will wear only stiff hats, or go about picking up cigar butts in order to appear men; or in the case of young girls who decide to become men, and bear themselves and dress themselves in a manner more appropriate to boys.

There are children who are said to have no imagination. This is surely an error. Either such children do not express themselves, or there are other reasons which compel them to take up battle against the appearance of fantasies. A child may contrive to feel a certain sense of power by suppressing his imagination. In a cramped striving to adjust to reality, these children believe that fantasy is unmanly or childlike, and refuse to partake in it; and there are cases in which this disinclination goes so far that their imagination seems totally lacking.

IV. Empathy and Identification

The soul has the faculty not only of perceiving what actually exists in reality, but also of feeling, of guessing, what will occur in the future. This is an important contribution to the function of pre-vision necessary to any easily mobile organism since such an organism is constantly faced with the problem of making adjustments. We call this faculty identification, or empathy. It is extraordinarily well developed in human beings. Its extent is so great that one finds it in every corner of the psychic life. The necessity for pre-vision is the prime condition of its existence. If we are forced to pre-view, to pre-judge, to presume how we should act if a certain situation were to occur, we must learn how to gain a sound judgment of a situation which has not yet occurred, through correlation of our thinking, feeling, and perception. It is essential to win a point of view so that we may either approach the new situation with more strenuous efforts, or avoid it with greater caution.

Empathy occurs in the moment one human being speaks with another. It is impossible to understand another individual if it is impossible at the same time to identify oneself with him. Drama is the artistic expression of empathy. Other examples of empathy are those cases in which someone has a strange feeling of uneasiness when he notices another in danger. This empathy may be so strong that one makes involuntary defense movements, even though there is no danger to oneself. We all know the well known gesture which is made when someone has dropped his glass! At a bowling alley one may see certain players following the course of the ball with movements of their body as though they wanted to influence its course by this movement! Similarly during football games whole sections of people in the grand stand will push in the direction of their favorite team, or make resistive pressure when the opponent team has the ball. A common expression is the involuntary application of imaginary brakes by the occupants of a motor car whenever they feel that they are in danger. Few people can pass a tall building in which someone is washing a window without experiencing certain contractions and defense movements. When a speaker loses his presence of mind and cannot proceed, people in the audience are oppressed and uneasy. In the theatre particularly we can hardly avoid identifying ourselves with the players, or prevent ourselves from acting the most varied rôles within ourselves. Our entire life is very much dependent upon the faculty of identification. If we seek for the origin of this ability to act and feel as if we were someone else, we can find it in the existence of an inborn social feeling. This is, as a matter of fact, a cosmic feeling and a reflection of the connectedness of the whole cosmos which lives in us; it is an inescapable characteristic of being a human being. It gives us the faculty of identifying ourselves with things which are quite outside our own body.

Just as there are various degrees of the social feeling so

there are various degrees of empathy. These may be observed even in childhood. There are children who occupy themselves with dolls just as though they were human beings, whereas others are more interested in seeing what is inside of them. By projecting the communal relationships from human beings to less valuable or lifeless objects, the development of an individual may be entirely stopped. Cases of cruelty to animals which we see in childhood were impossible without an almost total absence of the social feeling, and the ability to identify with other living beings. The consequences of this defect lead children to develop interest in things which are of very little value or significance for their development into fellow human beings. They think only of themselves, and lose all interest for the joys or woes of others. These are manifestations which are intimately related to a deficient degree of empathy. The inability to identify oneself with another may lead so far that an individual refuses entirely to cooperate with his fellow men.

V. Hypnosis and Suggestion

We may expect that children who feel themselves oppressed by their environment will show a deficient amenity to the influence of their educators. Cases occur, however, in which the external pressure is so strong that it removes all obstacles with the result that the authoritative influence is retained and obeyed. It is easy to prove that this obedience is sterile of all social good. It sometimes manifests itself in such a grotesque fashion that it renders the obedient individual unfit for life. By dint of their servile obedience such individuals are incapable of any action or thought without an appropriate command from someone else. The great danger which this far reaching submission carries in itself is to be measured by the fact that there are children who, when they develop into adults, obey anyone's commands, even to the commission of crimes.

Interesting examples are to be found in gangs. Those who carry out the gang's commands belong to this class, whereas the leader of the gang usually holds himself far from the scene of action. In almost every important criminal case dealing with a gang crime, some such servile man has been the cat's paw. This far-reaching blind obedience attains such unbelievable depths that we can occasionally find people who are actually proud of their servility, and find it a way to the satisfaction of their ambition.

If we limit ourselves to normal cases of mutual influence, we find that those people are most capable of being influenced, who are most amenable to reason and logic, those whose social feeling has been least distorted. On the contrary, those who thirst for superiority and desire domination are very difficult to influence. Observation teaches us this fact every day.

When parents complain about a child it is only very rarely that they do so because of his blind obedience. The most common complaint arises because of his disobedience. Examination shows that such children are caught in a current which would make them superior to their environment; they are striving to batter down the cramping walls of their little life. They have been made unapproachable for educational influence by virtue of a mistaken treatment at home.

The intensive striving for power is inversely proportional to the degree to which one can be educated. Despite this fact, our family education is concerned, for the most part, in spurring on the ambition of the child, and awakening ideas of grandeur in his mind. This does not occur because of thoughtlessness, but because our whole culture is permeated with similar grandiose delusions. In the family, as in our civilization, the greatest emphasis is placed upon that individual who is greater, and better, and more glorious, than all the others in his environment. In the chapter on vanity we shall have occasion to show how maladapted this method of education towards ambition is to the communal life, and how the development of the mind can be stunted by the difficulties which ambition places in its way.

Every medium is in a position similar to individuals who are influenced by every turn of their environment as a consequence of their unconditional obedience. Imagine obeying every whim that anyone voices, for a short time! Hypnosis is based upon a similar preparation. Anyone may say, or believe, that he has the will to be hypnotized, but the psychic readiness to submit may be wanting. A second individual may consciously resist, and still be innately desirous to submit. In hypnosis the psychic attitude of the medium alone determines his behavior. What he says, or what he believes, is of no consequence. Confusion over this fact has allowed much misinformation to grow up concerning hypnosis. In hypnosis one is usually occupied with individuals who *seem* to be striving against the hypnosis, but are essentially desirous of submitting to the demands of the hypnotizer. This readiness may have various boundaries so that the results of hypnosis differ in every individual. In no case does the degree of readiness to be hypnotized depend upon the will of the hypnotizer. It is conditioned entirely by the psychic attitude of the medium.

In its essence, hypnosis somewhat resembles sleep. It is mysterious only because this sleep may be produced at the command of another. The command is effective solely when it is given to someone who is willing to submit to it. The determining factors are, as usual, the nature and character of the medium or subject. Only that man who is willing to accede to the demands of another without the exercise of his critical faculties, is capable of producing a hypnotic sleep; the hypnosis is more than an ordinary sleep in that it excludes the faculty of movement to such a degree that even the motor centers are mobilized at the command of the hypnotizer. A certain twilight slumber is all that is left of normal sleep in this state, in which the subject can remember only those things which the hypnotizer allows him to remember. The most important fact in hypnosis is that our critical faculties, those finest products of the soul, are completely paralyzed during the hypnotic trance. The hypnotized subject becomes, so to speak, the elongated hand of the hypnotizer, an organ functioning at his command.

Most people who have the power of influencing the behavior of others ascribe this faculty to some mysterious power which is peculiar to them. This leads to an enormous amount of mischief, especially in the pernicious activities of the telepaths and hypnotizers. These gentlemen commit such arrant crimes against mankind that they are quite capable of utilizing any instrument appropriate to their nefarious purposes. This does not say that all the manifestations which they produce are based upon a swindle. The human animal, unfortunately, is capable of such submission that it falls victim to anyone who poses as the possessor of special powers. Only too many human beings have acquired the habit of recognizing an authority without testing it. The public wants to be fooled. It wants to swallow every bluff without subjecting it to rational examination. Such activity will never bring any order into the communal life of mankind but will lead only, again and again, to the revolt of those who have been imposed upon. No telepath nor hypnotizer has had luck with his experiments for any great length of time. Very frequently they have come in contact with someone, some so-called medium, who has fooled them for all he was worth. This has sometimes been the experience of important scientists who have attempted to show their powers on mediums.

There are other cases in which there is a curious admixture of truth and falsehood: the medium is, so to speak, a deceived deceiver, one who fools the hypnotizer in part, but also subordinates himself to his will. The power which apparently is at work here is never the power of the hypnotizer, but always the readiness of the medium to subordinate himself and submit. There is no magic power which influences the medium unless it be the ability of the hypnotizer to bluff. Any man who is accustomed to living rationally, who makes his own decisions, who does not swallow anyone's word uncritically, is naturally not to be hypnotized, and will, therefore, never be able to show any telepathic powers. Hypnosis and telepathy are only the manifestations of servile obedience.

At this point we must also consider suggestion. Suggestion can be best understood when one includes it in the category of impressions and stimuli. It is self-understood that no human being is stimulated only occasionally. All of us are constantly under the influence of innumerable impressions arising in the outer world. The mere perception of a stimulus never occurs. Once an impression is felt, it continues to exercise its effect. When these impressions take the form of the demands and the entreaties of another human being, his attempts at conviction or his arguments, we speak of suggestion. It is a case either of the transformation, or of the reinforcement, of a point of view which is already present in the person to whom the suggestions are made. The more difficult problem really begins with the fact that every human being reacts variously to stimuli coming from the external world. The degree to which he can be influenced is intimately connected with his independence. There are two types of human beings which we must bear in mind. One type always overvalues the other fellow's opinion and therefore values its own opinions only lightly, whether they are right or wrong. They are given to over-rating the importance of others, and to adapting themselves gladly to their opinions. These individuals are exceptionally susceptible to suggestion, or hypnosis. A second type considers every stimulus or suggestion as an insult. Here are the individuals who consider that only their own opinion is right, and are really not concerned as to its actual correctness, or incorrectness. They disregard anything originating in another human being. Both types carry with them a sense of weakness. The second type expresses this weakness by not being able to receive anything from another human being. Members of this category are usually very belligerent persons, although they may pride themselves upon being open to suggestions. They talk about this openness and reasonableness, however, only in order to reinforce their isolated position. Actually they cannot be approached, and it is very difficult to do anything with them.

CHAPTER V

THE FEELING OF INFERIORITY AND THE STRIVING FOR RECOGNITION

I. The Situation in Early Childhood

We are now certainly prepared to recognize the fact that children who have been treated as step-children by Nature have an entirely different attitude toward life and toward their fellow human beings than those to whom the joys of existence were vouchsafed at an early age. One can state as a fundamental law that children who come into the world with organ inferiorities become involved at an early age in a bitter struggle for existence which results only too often in the strangulation of their social feelings. Instead of interesting themselves in an adjustment to their fellows, they are continually preoccupied with themselves, and with the impression which they make on others. What holds good for an organic inferiority is as valid for any social or economic burden which might manifest itself as an additional load, capable of producing a hostile attitude toward the world. The deciding trend becomes determined at an early age. Such children frequently have a sentiment as early as their second year of life, that they are somehow not as adequately equipped for the struggle as their playmates; they sense that they dare not trust themselves to the common games and pastimes. As a result of past privations they have acquired a feeling of being neglected, which is expressed in their attitude of anxious expectation. One must remember that every child occupies an inferior position in life; were it not for a certain quantum of social feeling on the part of his family he would be incapable of independent existence. One realizes that the beginning of every life is fraught with a more or less deep feeling of inferiority when one sees the weakness and helplessness of every child. Sooner or later every child becomes conscious of his inability to cope single-handed with the challenges of existence. This feeling of inferiority is the driving force, the starting point from which every childish striving originates. It determines how this individual child acquires peace and security in life, it determines the very goal of his existence, and prepares the path along which this goal may be reached.

The basis of a child's educability lies in this peculiar situation which is so closely bound up with his organic potentialities. Educability may be shattered by two factors. One of these factors is an exaggerated, intensified, unresolved feeling of inferiority, and the other is a goal which demands not only security and peace and social equilibrium, but a striving to express power over the environment, a goal of dominance over one's fellows. Children who have such a goal are always easily recognized. They become "problem" children because they interpret every experience as a defeat, and because they consider themselves always neglected and discriminated against both by nature and by man. One need but consider all these factors to see with what compulsive necessity a crooked, inadequate, error-ridden development may occur in the life of a child. Every child runs the danger of a mistaken development. Every child finds itself in a situation which is precarious, at some time or another.

Since every child must grow up in an environment of adults he is predisposed to consider himself weak, small, incapable of living alone; he does not trust himself to do those simple tasks that one thinks him capable of doing, without mistakes, errors, or clumsinesses. Most of our errors in education begin at this point. In demanding more than the child can do, the idea of his own helplessness is thrown into his face. Some children are even consciously made to feel their smallness and helplessness. Other children are regarded as toys, as animated dolls; others, again, are treated as valuable property that must be carefully watched, while others still are made to feel they are so much useless human freight. A combination of these attitudes on the part of the parents and adults often leads a child to believe that there are but two things in his power, the pleasure or displeasure of his elders. The type of inferiority feeling produced by the parents may be further intensified by certain peculiar characteristics of our civilization. The habit of not taking children seriously belongs in this category. A child gets the impression that he is a nobody, without rights; that he is to be seen, not heard, that he must be courteous, quiet, and the like.

Numerous children grow up in the constant dread of being laughed at. Ridicule of children is well-nigh criminal. It retains its effect upon the soul of the child, and is transferred into the habits and actions of his adulthood. An adult who was continually laughed at as a child may be easily recognized; he cannot rid himself of the fear of being made ridiculous again. Another aspect of this matter of not taking children seriously is the custom of telling children palpable lies, with the result that the child begins to doubt not only his immediate environment but also to question the seriousness and reality of life.

Cases have been recorded of children who laughed continually at school, seemingly without reason, who when questioned, admitted that they thought school was one of their parents' jokes and not worth taking seriously!

II. Compensating for the Feeling of Inferiority; the Striving for Recognition and Superiority

It is the feeling of inferiority, inadequacy, insecurity, which determines the goal of an individual's existence. The tendency to push into the limelight, to compel the attention of parents, makes itself felt in the first days of life. Here are found the first indications of the awakening desire for recognition developing itself under the concomitant influence of the sense of inferiority, with its purpose the attainment of a goal in which the individual is seemingly superior to his environment.

The degree and quality of the social feeling helps to determine the goal of dominance. We cannot judge any individual, whether it is a child or adult, without drawing a comparison between his goal of personal dominance and the quantum of his social feeling. His goal is so constructed that its achievement promises the possibility either of a sentiment of superiority, or an elevation of the personality to such a degree that life seems worth living. It is this goal which gives value to our sensations, which links and coordinates our sentiments, which shapes our imagination and directs our creative powers, determines what we shall remember and what we must forget. We can realize how relative are the values of sensations, sentiments, affects, and imagination, when not even these are absolute quantities; these elements of our psychic activity are influenced by the striving for a definite goal, our very perceptions are prejudiced by it, and are chosen, so to speak, with a secret hint at the final goal toward which the personality is striving.

We orient ourselves according to a fixed point which we have artificially created, which does not in reality exist, a fiction. This assumption is necessary because of the inadequacy of our psychic life. It is very similar to other fictions which are used in other sciences, such as the division of the earth by non-existent, but highly useful meridians. In the case of all psychic fictions we have to do with the following: we assume a fixed point even though closer observation forces us to admit that it does not exist. The purpose of this assumption is simply to orient ourselves in the chaos of existence, so that we can arrive at some apperception of relative values. The advantage is that we can categorize every sensation and every sentiment according to this fixed point, once we have assumed it.

Individual Psychology, therefore, creates for itself a heuristic system and method: to regard human behavior and understand it as though a final constellation of relationships were produced under the influence of the striving for a definite goal upon the basic inherited potentialities of the organism. Our experience, however, has shown us that the assumption of a striving for a goal is more than simply a convenient fiction. It has shown itself to be largely coincident with the actual facts in its fundamentals, whether these facts are to be found in the conscious or unconscious life. The striving for a goal, the purposiveness of the psychic life is not only a philosophic assumption, but actually a fundamental fact.

When we question how we can most advantageously oppose the development of the striving for power, this most prominent evil of our civilization, we are faced with a difficulty, for this striving begins when the child cannot be easily approached. One can begin to make attempts at improvement and clarification only much later in life. But *living* with the child at this time does offer an opportunity to so develop his social feeling that the striving for personal power becomes a negligible factor.

A further difficulty lies in the fact that children do not express their striving for power openly, but hide it under the guise of charity and tenderness, and carry out their work behind a veil. Modestly, they expect to escape disclosure in this way. An uninhibited striving for power is capable of producing degenerations in the psychic development of the child, an exaggerated drive for security and might, may change courage to impudence, obedience into cowardice, tenderness into a subtle treachery for dominating the world. Every natural feeling or expression finally carries with it a hypocritical afterthought whose final purpose is the subjugation of the environment.

Education affects the child by virtue of its conscious or unconscious desire to compensate him for his insecurity, by schooling him in the technique of life, by giving him an educated understanding, and by furnishing him with a social feeling for his fellows. All these measures, whatever their source, are means to help the growing child rid himself of his insecurity and his feeling of inferiority. What happens in the soul of the child during this process we must judge by the character traits he develops since these are the mirror of the activity in his soul. The actual inferiority of a child, important as it is for his psychic economy, is no criterion of the weight of his feeling of insecurity and inferiority, since these depend largely upon his interpretation of them.

One cannot expect a child to have a correct estimation of himself in any particular situation; one does not expect it of adults! It is precisely here that difficulties grow apace. One child will grow up in a situation so complicated that errors concerning the degree of his inferiority are absolutely unavoidable. Another child will be able better to interpret his situation. But taken by and large the interpretation which the child has of his feeling of inferiority varies from day to day until it becomes consolidated, finally, and is expressed as a definite self-estimation; this becomes a "constant" of self-evaluation which the child retains, in all his conduct. According to this crystallized norm or "constant of self-estimation" the compensation trends which the child creates to guide him out of his inferiority will be directed toward this, or the other, goal.

The mechanism of the striving for compensation with which the soul attempts to neutralize the tortured feeling of inferiority has its analogy in the organic world. It is a well known fact that those organs of our body which are essential for life, produce an overgrowth, and over-function when their productivity is lessened through damage to their normal state. Thus in difficulties of circulation, the heart, seeming to draw its new strength from the whole body, may enlarge until it is more powerful than a normal heart. Similarly, the soul, under pressure of the feeling of inferiority, or the torturing thought that the individual is small and helpless, attempts with all its might to become master over this "inferiority complex."

When the feeling of inferiority is intensified to the degree that the child fears he will never be able to compensate for his weakness, the danger arises that in his striving for compensation he will be satisfied not with a simple restoration of the balance of power; he will demand an over-compensation, will seek an overbalance of the scales!

The striving for power and dominance may become so exaggerated and intensified that it must be called pathological. When this occurs the ordinary relationships of life will never be satisfactory. The movements in these cases are apt to have a certain grandiose gesture about them. They are well adapted to their goal. Where we are dealing with a pathological power-drive we find individuals who seek to secure their position in life with extraordinary efforts, with greater haste and impatience, with more violent impulses, and without consideration of any one else. These are the children whose actions become more noticeable because of their exaggerated movements towards their exaggerated goal of dominance; their attacks on the lives of others necessitate that they defend their own lives. They are against the world, and the world is against them.

This need not necessarily occur in the worst sense of the word. There are children who express the striving of power in a manner not calculated to bring them into immediate conflict with society, and their ambition may be considered as no abnormal characteristic. Yet when we carefully investigate their activity and achievements we find that society at large does not benefit from their triumphs, because their ambition is an asocial one. Their ambition will always put them in the path of other human beings as disturbing elements. Little by little, too, other characteristics will appear which, if we consider total human relationships, will assume an increasingly antisocial color.

In the forefront of these manifestations are pride, vanity, and the desire to conquer everyone at any price. The latter may be subtly accomplished by the relative elevation of the individual, by his deprecation of all those with whom he comes in contact. In the latter case the important thing is the "distance" which separates him from his fellows. His attitude is not only uncomfortable for the environment, but for the individual who practices it, because it continually brings him into contact with the dark side of life and prevents him from experiencing any joy in living.

The exaggerated drive for power with which some children wish to assure their prestige over their environment, soon forces them into an attitude of resistance against the ordinary tasks and duties of everyday life. Compare such a power-hungry individual with the ideal social being, and one can, after some little experience, specify, so to speak, his social index, that is, the degree to which he has removed himself from his fellow-man. A keen judge of human nature, keeping his eyes open to the value of physical defects and inferiorities, knows nevertheless that such character traits were impossible without antecedent difficulties in the evolution of his soul.

When we have gained a true knowledge of human nature, built upon a recognition of the value of the difficulties which may occur in the proper development of the soul, it can never be an instrument of harm so long as we have ourselves thoroughly developed our social feeling. We can but help our fellow-men with it. We must not blame the bearer of a physical defect, nor a disagreeable character trait, for his indignation. He is not responsible for it. We must indeed admit his right to be indignant to the last limits, and we must be conscious that we bear a part of the common blame for his situation. The blame belongs to us because we too have taken part in the inadequate precautions against the social misery which has produced it. If we stick to this standpoint we can eventually ameliorate the situation.

We approach such an individual not as a degraded, worthless outcast, but as a fellow human being; we give him an atmosphere in which he will find that there are possibilities for feeling himself the equal of every other human being in his environment. Think how unpleasant the sight of an individual's appearance, whose organ or bodily inferiorities are externally visible, may be to you! It is a good index of the amount of education you yourself need in order to come to an absolutely just sense of social values, and put yourself into complete harmony with the truth of the social feeling. And we can judge then, too, how much our civilization owes to such an individual.

It is self-understood that those who come into the world with organ inferiorities feel an added burden of existence from their earliest days, and, as a result, find themselves pessimistic as regards the whole matter of existence. Children in whom the feeling of inferiority has become intensified through some cause or other, although their organ inferiorities are not nearly so noticeable, find themselves in a similar situation. The feeling of inferiority may be so intensified artificially that the result is exactly the same as though the child came into the world greatly crippled. A very severe education during the critical period, for instance, may effect such an unfortunate result. The thorn which has been stuck into their side in the early days of their existence is never removed, and the coldness which they have experienced prevents them from approaching other human beings in their environment. They believe themselves thus in a world devoid of love and affection, with which they have no common point of contact.

An example: A patient, noticeable because he is continually telling us about his great sense of duty, and the importance of all his actions, lives with his wife in the worst possible relationship. Here are two individuals who measure the value of any event as a means toward the subjugation of their mate, to the thickness of a hair. Wrangling, reproaches, insults, in the course of which the two become entirely estranged from one another, are the inevitable result. What little social feeling for his fellow men the husband retains, at least so far as his wife and friends are concerned, is choked by his thirst for superiority.

We learn the following facts from the story of his life:— he was practically undeveloped physically until his seventeenth year. His voice was the voice of a young boy, he had no body or face hair, and he was among the smallest boys in his school. Today he is thirty-six. Nothing which is not entirely masculine is noticeable about his outer appearance, and Nature seemingly has caught up with herself and completed everything which she had hardly begun to fashion when he was seventeen. But for eight years he suffered from this failure of development, and at that time he had no guarantee that Nature would ever compensate for his anomalies. During this entire period he was tortured with the thought that he must always remain a "child."

At that early age the beginnings of his present character traits could be noted. He acted as though he were very important, and as if his every action had the utmost weight. Every movement served the purpose of bringing him into the center of attention. In the course of time he acquired those characteristics which we see in him today. After he married he was continually occupied with impressing his wife with the fact that he was really bigger and more important than she thought, while she was continually busied with showing him that his assertions concerning his value were untrue! Under these circumstances their marriage, which showed signs of disruption even during their engagement, could hardly develop favorably, and ended finally in a social cataclysm. The patient came to the physician at this time—since the break-up of his marriage served only to accentuate the dilapidation of his already battered self-esteem. To be cured, he had to learn first from the physician how to know human nature, he had to learn how to appreciate the error he had made in life. And this error, this wrong evaluation of his inferiority, had colored his entire life up to the time of his treatment.

CHAPTER VI

THE PREPARATION FOR LIFE

One of the fundamental tenets of Individual Psychology is that all the psychic phenomena can be considered as preparations for a definite goal. In the configuration of the soul life which we have previously described we can see a constant preparation for the future in which the wishes of the individual appear fulfilled. This is a general human experience and all of us must go through this process. All the myths, legends and sagas which speak of an ideal future state concern themselves with it. The convictions of all peoples that there was once a paradise, and the further echo of this process in the desire of humanity for a future in which all difficulties have been overcome, may be found in all religions. The dogma of the immortality of the soul, or its re-incarnation, is a definite evidence of the belief that the soul can arrive at a new configuration. Every fairy tale is a witness of the fact that the hope of a happy future has never failed in mankind.

I. Play

There is in the child life an important phenomenon which shows very clearly the process of preparation for the future. It is play. Games are not to be considered as haphazard ideas of parents or educators, but they are to be considered as educational aids and as stimuli for the spirit, for the fantasy, and for the life-technique of the child. The preparation for the future can be seen in every game. The manner in which a child approaches a game, his choice, and the importance which he places upon it, indicate his attitude and relationship to his environment and how he is related to his fellow men. Whether he is hostile or whether he is friendly, and particularly whether he has the tendency to be a ruler, is evident in his play; and in observing a child in his play we can see his whole attitude toward life. Play is of utmost importance to every child. The discovery of these facts which teach us that the play of children is to be considered as a preparation for the future is due to Gross, a professor of pedagogy, who discovered the same tendencies in the play of animals.

But we have not exhausted all the view points as to the nature of play, with the concept of preparation. Above all else games are communal exercises, they enable the child to satisfy and fulfill his social feeling. Children who evade games and play are always open to the suspicion that they have made a bad adjustment to life. These children gladly withdraw themselves from all games, or when they are put on the playground with other children usually spoil the pleasure of the others. Pride, deficient self-esteem and the consequent fear of playing one's rôle badly are the chief reasons for this behavior. In general by watching a child at play we shall be able to determine with great certainty the quantum of his social feeling.

The goal of superiority, another factor obvious in play, betrays itself in the child's tendency to be the commander and the ruler. We can discover this tendency by watching how the child pushes himself forward and to what degree he prefers those games which give him an opportunity to satisfy his desire to play the leading rôle. There are very few games which do not have at least one of these factors, preparation for life, social feeling, or the striving for domination, incorporated in them.

There is, however, one other factor which is present in play. It is the possibility that the child can express himself in a game. The child is more or less placed upon his own in play, and his performance is stimulated by his connection with the other children. There are a number of games which especially emphasize this creative bent. In the preparation for a future profession those plays which carry in themselves the possibility for the exercise of the creative spirit of the child are especially important. In the life histories of many people, it has happened that they have made dresses for dolls in their childhood, and later made dresses for adults.

Play is indivisibly connected with the soul. It is, so to speak, a kind of profession, and must be considered as such. Therefore, it is not an insignificant matter to disturb a child in his play. Play should never be considered as a method of killing time. In regard to the goal of preparing for the future, every child has in him something of the adult he will be at sometime. Thus in the appraisal of an individual we can draw our conclusions more easily when we have a knowledge of his childhood.

II. Attention and Distraction

Attention is one of the characteristics of the soul which is in the very forefront of human accomplishments. When we bring our sense organs to the consideration of some particular event outside or inside our person, we have a feeling of particular tension, which does not spread over our entire body, but is limited to a single sense organ, as for instance, the eye. We have the feeling that something is being prepared. In the case of the eye the direction of the ocular axis gives us this particular feeling of tension.

If attention calls forth a particular tension in any part of the soul or in our motor organism, then other tensions are at the same time excluded. Thus as soon as we wish to be attentive to any one thing we desire to exclude all other disturbances. Attention, so far as the soul is concerned, means an attitude of willingness to make a special bridge between ourselves and a definite fact, a preparation for offense, which grows out of our necessity, or out of an unusual situation which demands that our whole power be directed toward a particular purpose.

Every human being, if we exclude sickness and feeblemindedness, possesses the ability to pay attention, but inattentive persons are frequently found. There are a number of reasons for this. In the first place, fatigue or sickness are factors which influence the ability to pay attention. Further, there are other individuals whose deficient attention is due to the fact that they do not want to pay attention, because the object to which they should be attentive does not fit into their behavior pattern; on the other hand their attention immediately awakens when they are considering some matter which is germane to their style of life. A further reason for deficient attention is to be found in the tendency toward opposition. Children are very easily given to opposition, and it often happens that such children answer "No" to every stimulus which is offered them. It is necessary for their opposition to become open. It is the duty of the educator and of educational tact to reconcile such a child by relating the study which he must learn to his behavior pattern, and making it germane to his style of life.

Some see and hear and perceive every change. Some approach life entirely with their eyes; others entirely with their auditory apparatus. Some see nothing, take notice of nothing, and are not to be interested in visual things. We may find an individual inattentive when his situation would warrant his utmost interest because his more sensitive receptors are not stimulated.

The most important factor in the awakening of attention is a really deep rooted interest in the world. Interest lies in a much deeper psychic stratum than attention. If we have interest, then it is self-understood that we should also pay attention; and where interest exists, an educator need not concern himself with attention. It becomes a simple instrument with which one conquers a field of knowledge for a definite purpose. No one has ever developed without making mistakes in the process. It follows that the attention is likewise involved when some such mistaken attitude has become fixed in an individual, and it thus happens that attention is directed toward things which are not important in the preparation for life. When the *interest* is directed towards one's own body, or towards one's own power, one is *attentive* wherever these interests become involved, wherever there is something to be won, or wherever one's power is threatened. Attention can never be linked with something extraneous so long as some new interest is not substituted in place of the power interest. One can observe how children become immediately attentive when their recognition and significance are in question. Their attention on the other hand is easily extinguished when they have the feeling there is "nothing in it" for them.

A defective attention actually means nothing more than that a person prefers to withdraw from a situation, to which he is supposed to pay attention. It is incorrect, therefore, to say that someone cannot concentrate himself. It can easily be proved that he concentrates very well, but always on something else. Lack of will power and lack of energy are similar to the inability to concentrate. We usually find an obdurate will and an indomitable energy expressed in a different direction in these cases. Treatment is not simple. It can be attempted solely by changing the entire style of life of the individual. In every case we can be sure that we are dealing with a defect only because another goal is being pursued.

Not infrequently inattention becomes a permanent characteristic. We often meet individuals who have been given a definite task which they have declined to do, which they have only partially accomplished, or have fully evaded, with the result that they are always a burden to someone else. Their constant inattention is a fixed character trait, which appears as soon as they are under the necessity of doing something which is demanded of them.

III. Criminal Negligence and Forgetfulness

We usually speak of criminal negligence when the safety or health of an individual is threatened by neglect in the application of necessary precaution. Criminal neglect is a phenomenon which demonstrates the utmost degree of in-attention. Such defective attention is based on a defective interest for one's fellow men. One can determine whether children think only of themselves, or whether they take into consideration rights of others, by watching for traits of negligence in their games. Such phenomena are definite standards of the communal consciousness and the social feeling of a human being. When the social feeling has been insufficiently developed, one acquires sufficient interest for his fellows only with the greatest difficulty, even under threat of punishment; whereas in the presence of a well-developed community consciousness, this interest is self-evident.

Criminal neglect, therefore, amounts to a defective social feeling, yet we must not be too intolerant lest we forget to investigate why an individual does not possess the interest in his fellow-men which we might expect of him.

We can produce forgetfulness by setting limits to our attention, just as we can arrange the loss of valuables. Despite the presence of the possibility for greater tension—that is, interest—this interest may be so dampened by displeasure, that a loss or memory lapse is initiated, or at least facilitated thereby. Such is the case, for instance, when children lose their school books. It is always easy to prove that they have not yet become accustomed to their school surroundings. Housewives who are constantly losing or misplacing their keys are usually women who have never become friendly with their profession as housewife. Forgetful people usually prefer not to revolt openly, yet a certain lack of interest in their tasks is betrayed by their forgetfulness.

IV. The Unconscious

Our descriptions have often shown individuals who are not conscious of the meaning of the phenomena of their psychic life. Seldom will an attentive man be able to tell you why he sees everything at once. Certain psychic faculties are not to be sought in the realm of consciousness; although we can consciously force our attention to a certain degree, the stimulus to that attention lies not in consciousness, but in our interests, and these, again, lie for the most part in the sphere of the unconscious. Taken in its largest scope, this is at once an aspect and an important factor in the soul life. We may seek and find the behavior pattern of a man in the unconscious. In his conscious life we have but a reflection, a negative, to deal with. A vain woman usually has no knowledge of her vanity in most of the instances in which she exhibits it; quite to the contrary, she will behave so that only her modesty will be apparent to everyone. It is not necessary to know that one is vain to be vain. Indeed for the purposes of this woman, it would be quite futile for her to know that she is vain, since if she knew she were vain, she could not continue to be vain. We can acquire a certain dramatic security in not seeing anything of our own vanity solely by directing our attention to something extraneous or irrelevant. The whole process takes place in the dark. Attempt to talk to a vain man about his vanity and you will find it very difficult to achieve a conversation on the subject. He may show a tendency to evade the matter, to circumlocute, lest he be disturbed; this can but make us more certain of our opinion. He wants to play his little game, and immediately assumes a defensive attitude when some one inadvertently attempts to lift the veil from his little trick.

Human beings may be differentiated into two types; those who know more concerning their unconscious life than the average, and those who know less; that is, according to the extent of their sphere of consciousness. In a great many cases, we will find coincidently that an individual of the second type concentrates upon a small sphere of activity, whereas the individuals of the first type are connected with a many-sided sphere, and have large interests in men, things, events, and ideas. Those individuals who feel themselves pushed to the wall will naturally satisfy themselves with a small section of life, since they are foreign to life, and cannot see its problems with as much clarity as those who are playing the game according to the rules. They make bad team-mates. They will not be so capable of understanding the finer things of life. Because of their very limited interest in living, they perceive but an insignificant segment of its problems for the reason that they fear a broader view would be synonymous with a loss of personal power. As to individual occurrences in life, we can often discover that an individual knows nothing of his capabilities of living, because he undervalues himself. We will find also that he is not sufficiently oriented concerning his short-comings; he will consider himself a good man, whereas in reality, he does everything out of egoism; or vice-versa, he will consider himself an egoist in instances in which a closer analysis shows him to be a very good person indeed. It really does not matter what you think of yourself, or what other people think of you. The important thing is the general attitude toward human society, since this determines every wish and every interest and every activity of each individual.

We are dealing again with two types of human beings.

In the first class are those who live a more conscious life, who approach the problems of life without blinders on their eyes, in an objective manner. The second class approaches life with a prejudiced attitude, and sees only a small part of it. The behavior and speech of individuals of this type are always directed in an unconscious manner. Two human beings living with one another may find difficulties in life because one of them is constantly in opposition. This is not an uncommon occurrence. It is perhaps even less uncommon that both parties are in opposition. Each party knows nothing about his opposition, believes himself right, and give arguments to show that he is the champion of peace and harmony. The facts nevertheless belie his words. In actuality it is impossible for him to say a single word without attacking his partner on the flank with an opposing remark, albeit his attack is externally unnoticeable. On closer inspection we find that he has given himself up to a hostile and belligerent attitude throughout his life.

Human beings develop powers in themselves which are constantly at work, though they know nothing of them. These faculties lie hidden in the unconscious, influence their lives and occasionally lead to bitter consequences when they are not discovered. Dostoyevsky described such a case so beautifully in his novel *The Idiot* that it has been the marvel of psychologists ever since: during a social gathering a lady cautions the duke who is the hero of the novel, not to upset an expensive Chinese vase which stands near him, in a taunting tone. The duke assures her that he will take care, but a few minutes later the vase lies on the ground, shattered into pieces. No one in the group saw a mere accident in this occurrence; everyone felt it was a very consequent action, quite in keeping with the whole character of this man who felt himself insulted by the lady's words.

In judging a human being we must not be guided solely

by his conscious actions and expressions. Often little details in his thinking and behavior of which he is not conscious will give us a better clue to his real nature.

People for instance who practice such unpleasant activities as nail-biting or nose-boring do not know that they betray the fact that they are stubborn human beings in doing so, since they do not understand the relationships which have led them to these traits. Yet it is perfectly clear to us that a child must have been scolded repeatedly because of these habits; if, then, he does not give them up, despite the scoldings, he must be a stubborn human being! Were we more expert in our observation, we would have to draw very far reaching conclusions concerning any human being, by watching for such insignificant details, in which his whole being is mirrored.

These two following cases will show how important it is to the psychic economy that events which are unconscious, remain in the unconscious. The human soul has the capability of directing the consciousness, that is, of making conscious that which is necessary from the standpoint of some psychic movement, and vice-versa, to allow something to remain in the unconscious or make it unconscious, whenever this would seem advisable for the maintenance of the individual's behavior pattern.

The first case is that of a young man, a firstborn son, who grew up with a younger sister; his mother died when he was ten years old, and from that time his father, who was a very intelligent, well-meaning, ethical man, had to be the educator. The father spent most of his efforts developing his son's ambition and spurring him on to greater activity. The boy tried to be the leader in his classes, developed himself extraordinarily well, and so far as his ethical and scientific qualities were concerned, always took first place, much to the joy of his father, who expected him to play an important rôle in life, from the very first.

In the course of time this young man developed certain

traits which caused his father sorrow, and these he tried to change. The boy's sister grew up to be his obdurate rival. She also developed very well, although she was satisfied with utilizing the weapons of weakness for her triumphs, while she enlarged her significance at the cost of her brother. She had acquired a considerable facility in household tasks, which made competition difficult for her brother. As a boy, he found it very difficult to achieve, in domesticity, that recognition and significance which he had so easily won in other fields of endeavor. The father soon noticed that his son was acquiring a peculiar social life, which became the more evident as his puberty approached. As a matter of fact he had no social life. He was hostile to all new acquaintance-ships and where these acquaintanceships concerned girls, he simply ran away. At first his father saw nothing extraordinary in this, but as time went on the boy's social reactions acquired such dimensions that he hardly went out of the house, and even little walks, except in the late twilight, were unpleasant to him. He became so shut in that he refused, finally, to greet even his old acquaintances, although his attitude in school and towards his father remained beyond criticism.

When it had gone so far that no one could bring him anywhere, the father brought this boy to the physician. A few consultations sufficed to discover the cause of the difficulty. This boy believed that his ears were small and that therefore everyone considered him very ugly. As a matter of fact this was not the case. When his objection was overruled and he was told that his ears were in no-wise different from those of other boys, and it was shown him that he was using this as an excuse to withdraw from the company of human beings, he added further that his teeth and his hair also were ugly. This also was not the case.

On the other hand it was easily discovered that he was inordinately ambitious. He was well aware of his ambition and believed that his father, who had constantly stimulated him to greater and greater activity so that he might achieve a high position in life, had produced this trait in him. His plans for the future came to their climax in his desire to play the rôle of a hero of science. This would not be so remarkable were it not that with it was combined a tendency to avoid all the obligations of humanity and fellowship. Why did this boy make use of such very childish arguments? Had these arguments been right they might have justified him in approaching life with a certain caution and anxiety, because it is undoubtedly true that an ugly man encounters many difficulties in our civilization.

Further examination showed that this boy followed a particular goal with his great ambition. Formerly he had always been the first one in his class and he wanted to remain the first one. To achieve such a goal one has certain instruments such as concentration, industry and the like, at hand. These were not enough for him. He attempted to exclude everything which seemed unnecessary, out of his life. He might have expressed himself somewhat like this: "Since I am going to become famous and since I am going to dedicate myself entirely to my scientific labors, I must exclude all social relationships as unnecessary."

But he neither said nor thought this. On the contrary he took the unessential element of his alleged ugliness and utilized it for the attainment of his purpose. The elevation of this insignificant fact acquired value in his scheme of things in that it justified him in doing what in reality he wanted to do. All he needed to do now was to have courage to argue falsely, to exaggerate his ugliness, in order to pursue his secret purpose. Had he said that he wished to live like an ascetic hermit in order to attain his goal of being the first, his argument would have been transparent to everyone. Although unconsciously he was dedicated to the idea of playing the heroic rôle, he was consciously unaware of his purpose.

That he wished to hazard everything else in life and

gain this one point had never entered his head. If he had taken this into his consciousness and decided openly to stake everything in life in order to become a scientific hero, he could not have been as sure of himself as if he were to accomplish his purpose by saying that he was an ugly man and dared not go into society; in addition anyone who would say openly that he wanted forever to be first and the greatest, and was willing to sacrifice all human relationships for the sake of his goal, would make himself ridiculous in the eyes of his fellows. It would be too fearful a thought, a thought which one dared not think. There are certain ideas which one cannot hold too openly, both for the sake of others and for the sake of oneself. For this reason the guiding idea of this boy's life had to remain in his unconscious.

If now we make obvious to such an individual the mainsprings of his life, and demonstrate to him tendencies which he dared not look at in himself lest he lose his behavior pattern, we naturally disturb his entire psychic mechanism. What this individual has been trying at all costs to prevent, now happens! His unconscious thought processes become clear and transparent! Thoughts which were not to be thought, ideas which one dared not retain, tendencies which, if conscious, would disturb our entire behavior, are laid bare. It is a universal and human phenomenon that everyone seizes upon those thoughts which justify him in his attitude and rejects every idea which might prevent him from going on. Human beings dare only those things which in their interpretation of the world are valuable to them. That which is helpful we are conscious of; whatever can disturb our arguments we push into the unconscious.

The second case is the history of a very capable young boy whose father, a teacher, constantly spurred his son on to be the first in his class. In this case, too, the early days of this child were a series of victories. Wherever he appeared he was always the conqueror. He was one of the most charming members of his society and he had several close friends.

A great change occurred in his eighteenth year. He lost all his pleasure in life, was depressed, distracted, and went to great lengths to withdraw from the world. No sooner would he make a friendship than he broke it. Everyone found a stumbling block in his behavior. His father however hoped that his shut-in life would enable him to dedicate himself more intensely to his studies.

During the treatment of this boy he complained constantly that his father had robbed him of all joy in life, that he could find no self-confidence nor courage to go on with life, and that there was nothing left for him to do but to sorrow through the rest of his days in solitude. His progress in his studies had already become slower and he was failing in College. He explained that the change in his life had begun on the occasion during a social gathering in which his ignorance of modern literature had made him the object of ridicule among his friends. The repetition of similar experiences caused him to begin his isolation and gave him occasion to assume a position outside society. He was ruled by the idea that his father was to blame for his misfortune, and their relationship became worse day by day.

These two cases are similar to each other in many respects. In the first case our patient was shipwrecked on the resistance of his sister, whereas in the second it was the belligerent attitude toward a father who was at fault. Both patients were led on by an idea which we have been accustomed to call the heroic ideal. Both of them had become so intoxicated with their heroic ideal that they had lost all contact with life, had become discouraged and would have liked nothing better than to withdraw entirely from the struggle. But we cannot believe that our second boy would ever have said to himself: "Since I cannot continue this heroic existence I shall withdraw from life and embitter the rest of my days!"

To be sure, his father was wrong and his education was bad. It was quite evident that he had eyes for nothing but his bad education, of which he constantly complained, since he wanted to justify himself in his withdrawal, by assuming that his education had been so bad that withdrawal from society alone remained a solution of his problem. In this way he achieved a situation in which he suffered no more defeats, and he was able to credit his father with the total blame for his misfortune. Only in this way was he able to save a fraction of his self-esteem for himself and satisfy his striving for significance. He had a glorious past and his future triumphs had been stopped only by the fatal fact that his father, because of his bad pedagogy, had hindered him from developing to even more brilliant accomplishments.

In a way we might say that something like this train of thought remained unconsciously in his mind: "Since I now stand closer to the firing front of life, and since I realize that it will no longer be so easy always to be the first, I shall make every effort to withdraw entirely from life." Yet such an idea is clearly unthinkable. No one could say such a thing, but an individual can act *as if* he had taken this thought to heart. This is accomplished by making use of still further arguments; by busying himself entirely with the educational mistakes of his father he succeeds in evading society, and avoids all necessary decisions in life. Had this train of thought become conscious to him his secret behavior would, of necessity, have been disturbed. Therefore it remained unconscious. How could anyone say that he was an untalented human being when he had such a glorious past? To be sure none could blame him now if he succeeded to no new triumphs! The pernicious influence of his father's educational efforts was not to be laid aside. The son was judge, claimant, and defendant all in his own person. Should he now give up such a favorable position? He knew too well that his father was to blame only so long as

he, the son, wanted it, so long as he plied the lever which he
held between his hands.

V. Dreams

It has long been maintained that one could draw conclusions concerning the personality-as-a-whole from the
dreams of an individual. Lichtenberg, a contemporary of
Goethe, once said that one could guess the character and
essence of a human being better from his dreams than from
his actions and words. This is saying a little too much. We
have the standpoint that one must utilize *single* phenomena
of the psychic life with the greatest care and only in connection with other phenomena. We therefore will draw
conclusions concerning his character from the dreams of an
individual only when we can find additional supporting
evidence in other characteristics, to substantiate our interpretation of the dream.

If we busy ourselves with dreams as a means of approaching and learning something of the human soul, we shall
hardly view the problem from the standpoint of those investigators who seek in the dream and in dream interpretation fantastic and supernatural influences. We shall depend
upon the evidence of dreams only when we can be justified
and strengthened in our assertions by other far reaching
observations.

The tendency to believe that dreams have a particular
meaning for the future, persists even today. There are ideal-
ists who go so far as to allow themselves to be influenced
by their dreams. In this way one of our patients tricked
himself into avoiding every honorable occupation and devoted himself to gambling on the Exchange. He always
gambled according to dreams which he had. He had col-
lected historical evidence to prove he had always had
misfortune whenever he did not follow one of his dreams.

To be sure, he would dream of nothing except that which was the object of his constant waking attention. In this way he patted himself on the back, so to speak, in his dream, and was enabled for a considerable period of time to say that he had won very much under the influence of his dream. Some time later he explained that he placed no value whatever upon his dreams. It seems that he had lost all his money. Since this happens frequently to stock market operators even without dreams we see no miracle at work here. An individual who is intensely interested in some particular task is pursued by the necessity of solving this problem even at night. Some people do not sleep at all and constantly follow their problem while awake, others sleep but busy themselves with their plans in their dreams.

This peculiar phenomenon which occupies our thoughts during our sleep, is nothing more than the bridge from yesterday to tomorrow. If we know what attitude an individual takes towards life in general, how he bridges from the "now" into the "then," as a rule we will be able to understand also the peculiarities of his bridge structure in his dreams and be able to make valid conclusions from it. In other words it is the general attitude toward life which is at the basis of all dreams.

A young woman has the following dream: she dreams that her husband has forgotten her wedding anniversary and she reproaches him for it. This dream may mean several things. If such a problem can occur at all it immediately shows us that this marriage is marked by certain difficulties; the wife feels herself neglected. She explains however that she also forgot about the wedding anniversary but it was *she* who finally remembered it whereas her husband had to be reminded of it by her. She is the "better half." To a further question she said that actually nothing like this has ever happened and that her husband has always remembered the wedding anniversary. Therefore in the dream we see her tendency to be anxious for the future: something

like this *might* happen. We can further conclude that she is
given to making reproaches, to using arguments which are
intangible, and to nagging her husband for things which
might occur.

Still we could not be sure of our interpretation if we
did not have other evidence at hand which would reinforce
our conclusions. Asked about her earliest childhood remembrance, this woman narrated an event which had always
remained in her memory. When she was a three year old
child her aunt presented her with a carved wooden spoon
of which she was very proud; but once as she was playing
with it, it fell in a brook and floated away. She sorrowed
about this event for many days in such a way that everyone
in her environment was concerned with it.

The dream might lead us to assume that she was now
again thinking of the possibility that her marriage also
might float away from her. What if her husband *should*
forget about her wedding anniversary?

Another time she dreamt that her husband led her up into
a high building; the stairs grow more and more steep. Thinking that she has perhaps climbed too high she becomes ter-
ribly dizzy, has an attack of anxiety, and faints. One may
experience a similar sensation during the waking life, especially if one suffers from dizziness in high places in which
the fear is less that of the height than of the depth. By connecting the second dream with the first one and melting
them together the thought, feeling, and content of these
dreams give a clear impression that this is a woman who
is anxious about falling, who is afraid of mischief or
calamity. We can imagine that the waning affection of her
husband, or something similar, would be such a calamity.
What would happen if her husband in some way were not
compatible? What if their married life were disturbed?
Scenes might occur, fights take place, which might end with
the wife's fainting as though lifeless. This actually occurred
once during a family argument!

Now we come nearer to the meaning of the dream. It is quite a matter of indifference in which material the thought and emotional content of the dreams expresses itself, or what instruments are used for this expression, so long as the material is in any way useful and *some* expression is assured. In the dream the life problem of an individual is expressed in a simile. It is as though she said, "Do not climb too high so that you will not fall too far!" It may be well to recall the reproduction of a dream in the "Marriage Song" of Goethe. A knight comes home from the country and finds his castle deserted. Tired out he falls into his bed and in his dream he sees little figures coming out from under his bed and notices a marriage ceremony among these dwarfs. He is agreeably pleased by his dream. It is as though he wanted to corroborate in his thoughts the need for finding a woman. What he saw here in miniature occurred later in reality as he celebrated his own marriage.

We find many well known elements in this dream. In the first place the preoccupation of the poet with his own marriage is hidden behind it. We can see further how the dreamer, in his utter need strikes an attitude toward his contemporary situation in life. This situation demands marriage. He occupies himself in his dream with the problem of marriage and on the following day decides that it would be better if he too, were to get married.

Now let us consider a dream of a twenty-eight-year-old man. The movement of the dream, changing from ascent to descent like the temperature curve of a fever, indicates very clearly the psychic movements with which the life of this man is filled. The feeling of inferiority from which arise the tendencies and strivings for power and for dominance are easily recognized. He relates: "I am making an excursion with a large group of people. We must get out at a way-station because the ship on which we are to make this excursion is too small, and we must stay in this town over night. During the night the report comes that the ship is sinking, and all participants in the excursion are called to man the pumps in order to prevent it. I remember that I have some valuables in my baggage and rush to the ship where everyone else is already working at the pumps. I seek to escape this work and look for the baggage room. I succeed in fishing my knapsack through the window and at the same time I see a penknife which I like very much next to my knapsack. I put it in the knapsack. With an acquaintance I jump off as the ship sinks deeper and deeper. We jump off into the sea and land on the ground. Since the pier is too high we wander further along and come to a precipitous cliff down which I must go. I slide down. I have not seen my companion since leaving the ship. I go faster and faster and fear that I will be killed. Finally I land at the bottom and fall just in front of an acquaintance. It is an otherwise unknown young man who had been in a strike and had worked very quietly among the strikers, who was agreeable to me. He greets me with reproachful words, just as though he knew that I had left the others on the ship in the lurch. 'What are *you* doing here?' he asks. I seek to escape from this abyss which is surrounded on all sides by precipitous cliffs from which ropes hang down. I do not dare use them because they are too thin. With every attempt to climb out of the abyss I always slide back again. Finally I am on top, but I don't know how I got there. It seems to me that I purposely did not want to dream this part of the dream, as if I wanted to skip over it impatiently. On the edge of the abyss, on top, there was a road which was protected on the side of the abyss by a fence. People were going by here, and greeted me in a friendly fashion."

If we go back into the life of this dreamer the first thing that we hear is that he constantly suffered from severe illness up to the fifth year of his life, and that after this time he was often ill. As a result of his weak health he was carefully and anxiously guarded by his parents. His contact with other children was very slight. When he wanted to make contact with grown-ups he was always told by his parents that children should be seen and not heard, and that children do not belong with adults. He thus failed at a very early age to find those points of contact which are necessary for social life, and remained in connection solely with his parents. The further outcome of this was that he remained considerably behind his companions of the same age, with whom he could not keep up. We are not to be astonished to hear that he was also considered stupid among them, and soon became the butt of all their jokes. This circumstance, again, prevented him from finding friends.

An extraordinary feeling of inferiority was accentuated to the highest degree by these circumstances. His education was directed entirely by his well-wishing, but very irascible, military father, and by his weak, uncomprehending, very domineering mother. Although his parents were constantly reiterating their good will, his education must have been a very strict one. His discouragement played a considerable rôle in this process. A very significant event retained in his earliest childhood remembrances was that when he was but three years old his mother made him kneel on peas for half an hour. The reason for this was a disobedience whose cause his mother knew very well, as the child had told her. He had become frightened of a horseman and had therefore refused to run an errand for his mother. As a matter of fact he was spanked very seldom, but when this did occur, he was always beaten with a many-tailed dog whip, and never without being under the necessity of afterwards begging for forgiveness and relating the causes for which he had been beaten. "The child should know," said the father, "how he has misbehaved." Once he was beaten unjustly and as he could not say afterwards why he was beaten, was beaten again, indeed was beaten until he confessed to some misdeed or other.

A belligerent feeling towards his parents was present from his earliest days. His feeling of inferiority had acquired such dimensions that he could not even conceive of being superior. His life at school as well as at home was an almost unbroken chain of greater or lesser defeats. The smallest victory, in his opinion, was denied him. At school, up to the time that he was eighteen years old, he was always the one who was laughed at. Once he was laughed at even by his teacher, who read a bad theme aloud to the class and accompanied the reading with derisive remarks.

Everyone of these occurrences forced him further and further into isolation, and sooner or later he began to withdraw from the world, of his own accord. In his battle with his parents he happened upon a very effective although costly method of attack. He refused to speak, and with this gesture, he relinquished the most important grappling hook with which one fastens himself to the outer world. Since he was unable to speak with anyone, he became entirely solitary. Misunderstood by all, he spoke to none, particularly not with his parents; and finally no one addressed him. Every attempt to bring him into society came to grief, as every attempt to establish love relationships later in his life also failed, much to his sorrow. This is the course of his life until his twenty-eighth year. The deep inferiority complex which had permeated his whole spirit had as a consequence given rise to an ambition beyond all reason, an unreined striving for significance and superiority which ceaselessly distorted his feeling of human fellowship. The less he spoke, the more was his psychic life filled, by day and by night, with dreams of triumphs and victories of every sort.

And thus he dreamt one night the dream which we have related above, in which we see clearly the movement and the pattern according to which his psychic life developed. In conclusion let us recall a dream which Cicero has related, one of the most famous prophetic dreams in literature.

The poet Simonides, who at one time had found the corpse of an unidentified man lying on the street and had cared for his decent interment, was warned by the ghost of this dead man, as he was about to attempt a sea journey, that if he should take the journey he would be shipwrecked. Simonides did not go and all those who did, died.[1]

According to the report this event in connection with the dream is supposed to have had an unusually deep impression on all people for hundreds of years.

If we want to interpret this occurrence we must maintain that in that time ships were wrecked very frequently, and also that because of this reason many people who were on the eve of a sea journey, dreamt of shipwrecks, and that among these many dreams this particular dream demonstrated a particular coincidence between dream and reality which was so remarkable that it remained for posterity. It is quite conceivable that those who have a tendency to ferret out mysterious relationships have an especial weakness for just such stories, whereas we very calmly and soberly interpret the dream as follows: our poet probably never showed any great desire to take this trip because of his considerable care for his bodily well-being; as the hour of decision neared he was hard put to it to find a justification for his hesitating attitude. For this reason he allowed the corpse who was under the necessity of proving himself grateful for his decent burial, to appear in a prophetic rôle. That he now did not take the trip is self-understood. If the ship had not gone under the world would never have learned anything about the dream nor the story, in all probability. For we experience only those things which set our brain into unrest, which demonstrate to us that there is more wisdom hidden between heaven and earth than we allow ourselves to dream of. We can understand the prophetic nature of dreams in so far as we know that both dream and reality contain the same attitude toward life which an individual shows.

[1] Cf. Enne Nielson, "The Unexplained, In Its Course Through The Centuries." Published by the Langewies che-Brandt. Ebenhausen near Munich.

Another thing which we must consider is the fact that all dreams are not so easily understood; as a matter of fact only a very few are. We forget the dream immediately after it has left its peculiar impression and do not understand what is behind it unless we have been versed in the interpretation of dreams. Yet these dreams, too, are but a symbolic and metaphoric reflection of the activity and behavior pattern of an individual. The main meaning of a simile or comparison is that it affords us access to a situation in which we are anxious to find ourselves. If we are occupied with the solution of a problem and if our personality points a specific direction of approach, then we need but seek for an animating push to propel us into it. The dream is extraordinarily well suited to intensify an emotion, or produce the verve which is necessary to the solution of a particular situation. Nothing is altered by the fact that the dreamer does not understand the connection. It suffices that he finds the material and the boost in some fashion; the dream itself will give evidence of the manner in which the thought processes of the dreamer express themselves, as it will indicate the behavior pattern of the dreamer. The dream is like a column of smoke which shows that a fire is burning somewhere. The experienced woodsman can observe the smoke and tell what kind of wood is burning, just as the psychiatrist can draw conclusions concerning the nature of an individual by interpreting his dream.

Summing up, we can say that a dream shows not only that the dreamer is occupied in the solution of one of his life's problems, but also how he approaches these problems. In particular, those two factors which influence the dreamer in his relationship with the world and reality, the social feeling and the striving for power, will make themselves evident in his dream.

VI. Talent

Among those psychic phenomena which enable us to judge an individual we have left out of consideration one which is concerned with his intellectual powers. We have placed little value upon what an individual says or thinks of himself. We are convinced that each of us can somehow go astray and that each of us feels himself under the necessity of retouching his psychic image for his fellow man, through various of the complicated egoistic, moral, or other tricks. One thing we are, however, permitted to do, and that is to draw certain conclusions from specific thought processes and their expression in speech, even though this is possible only to a limited degree. We cannot exclude thought and speech from our examination if we wish to judge the individual correctly.

What we are pleased to call talent, that is the special ability to make judgments, has been the subject of numerous observations, analyses, and tests, among which the tests of intelligence, in children and adults, are well known. These are the so-called tests for talent. Up to the present time these tests have been unsuccessful. Whenever a number of pupils are tested the results usually show what the teacher could easily have determined without tests. In the beginning the experimental psychologists were very proud of this although it must have been evident at the same time that the tests were, to a certain degree, superfluous. Another objection to intelligence tests is the fact that the thought and judgment processes and abilities of children do not develop regularly, so that many children who show poor results on the tests, suddenly show an extraordinarily good development and talent after a few years. Another element which must be considered is that children in large cities, and those from certain social circles, are better prepared for the tests by virtue of their broader life. Their seemingly greater intelligence is deceptive and places other children who have not such a fund of preparation, relatively in the shadow. It is well known that eight to ten-year-old children of well-to-do families, are much more quick witted than poor children of the same age. This does not mean that the children of the wealthy are more talented but that the cause for this difference lies entirely in the circumstances of their previous life.

CHAPTER VII

SEX

I. Bisexuality and the Division of Labor

From our previous considerations we have learned that two great tendencies dominate all psychic phenomena. These two tendencies, the social feeling, and the individual striving for power and domination, influence every human activity and color the attitude of every individual in his striving for security, in his fulfillment of the three great challenges of life: love, work, and society. We shall have to accustom ourselves, in judging psychic phenomena, to investigate the quantitative and the qualitative relationships of these two factors if we want to understand the human soul. The relationship of these factors to one another conditions the degree to which anyone is capable of comprehending the logic of communal life, and therefore, the degree to which he is capable of subordinating himself to the division of labor which grows out of the necessity of that communal life.

Division of labor is a factor in the maintenance of human society which must not be overlooked. Everyone at some time, or at some place, must contribute his quota. That man who does not deliver his quota, who denies the value of communal life, becomes an anti-social being, and resigns his fellowship in humanity. In simple cases of this sort we speak of egotism, of mischievousness, of self-centeredness, of nuisance. In the more complicated cases, we see the eccentrics, the hoboes, and the criminals. Public condemnation of these traits and characteristics grows out of an appreciation of their origins, an intuition of their incompatibility with the demands of social life. Any man's value, therefore, is determined by his attitude toward his fellow men, and by the degree in which he partakes of the division of labor which communal life demands. His affirmation of this communal life makes him important to other human beings, makes him a link in the great chain which binds society, the chain which we cannot in any way disturb without also disturbing human society. A man's capabilities determine his place in the total production of human society. Much confusion has clouded this simple truth, because the striving for power and the lust for dominance have introduced false values into the normal division of labor. This striving for dominance has disturbed and thwarted the total production, and has given us a false basis for the judgment of human values.

Individuals have disturbed this division of labor by refusing to adapt themselves to the place that they must fill. Further, difficulties have arisen out of the false ambition and power wishes of individuals who have blocked communal life and the communal work for their own egoistic interests. Similarly, entanglements have been caused by class differences in our society. Personal power or economic interest have influenced the division of the field of labor by reserving all the better positions for individuals of certain classes, that is, those affording the greater power, while other individuals, of other classes, have been excluded from them. The recognition of these numerous factors in the structure of society enables us to understand why the division of labor has never proceeded smoothly. Forces continually disturbing this division of labor have created privilege for one, and slavery for another.

The bisexuality of the human race conditions another division of labor. Woman, by virtue of her physical constitution, is excluded from some certain activities, while on the other hand, there are certain labors which are not given to man, because man could better be employed at other tasks. This division of labor should have been instituted according to an entirely unprejudiced standard, and all the movements for the emancipation of women in so far as they have not overstepped logical points in the heat of conflict, have taken up the logic of this point of view. A division of labor is far from robbing woman of her femininity, or disturbing the natural relationships between man and woman. Each acquires those opportunities of labor which are best fitted for him. In the course of human development this division of labor has so configured itself that woman has taken over a certain part of the world's work (which might otherwise occupy a man too), in return for which man is in the position to use his powers to greater effect. We cannot call this division of labor senseless so long as the powers for work are not misused, and so long as physical and mental powers are not deflected to a bad end.

II. The Dominance of the Male in the Culture of Today

As a consequence of the development of culture in the direction of personal power, especially through the efforts of certain individuals and certain classes of society, who wish to secure privileges for themselves, this division of labor has fallen into characteristic channels which have colored our entire civilization. The importance of the male in the culture of today is greatly emphasized as a result. The division of labor is such that the privileged group, men, are guaranteed certain advantages, and this as a result of their domination over women in the division of labor. Thus the dominant male assumes advantages and directs the activity of women to the end that the more agreeable forms of life shall appertain always to the males, whereas those activities are allowed women which men can advantageously avoid.

As things stand now there is a constant striving on the part of men to dominate women, and an appropriate dissatisfaction with masculine domination on the part of women. Since the two sexes are so narrowly connected it is easily conceivable that this constant tension leads to psychic dissonances and to far reaching physical disturbances which must of necessity be extraordinarily painful to both sexes.

All our institutions, our traditional attitudes, our laws, our morals, our customs, give evidence of the fact that they are determined and maintained by privileged males for the glory of male domination. These institutions reach out into the very nurseries and have a great influence upon the child's soul. A child's understanding of these relationships need not be very great, but we must admit that his emotional life is immensely affected by them. These attitudes may well be investigated when for instance we see a young boy responding to the request to put on girls' clothes, with a terrific temper tantrum. Once let a boy's craving for power reach a certain degree, and you will surely find him showing a preference for the privileges of being a man which, he recognizes, guarantee his superiority everywhere. We have already mentioned the fact that the education in our families nowadays is only too well designed to overvalue the striving for power. The consequent tendency to maintain and exaggerate the masculine privilege follows naturally, for it is usually the father who stands as the family symbol of power. His mysterious comings and goings arouse the interest of the child much more than the constant presence of a mother. The child quickly recognizes the prominent rôle his father plays, and notes how he sets the pace, makes all arrangements, and appears everywhere as the leader. He sees how all obey his commands and how his mother asks him for his advice. From every angle, his father seems to be the one who is strong and powerful. There are children for whom the father is so much a standard that they believe that everything he says must be holy; they attest to the rightness of their views simply by saying that their father once said so. Even in those cases in which the fatherly influence does not seem to be so well marked, children will get the idea of the domination of the father because the whole load of the family seems to rest upon him, whereas, as a matter of fact, it is only the division of labor which enables the father in the family to use his powers to better advantage.

So far as the history of the origin of masculine dominance is concerned, we must call attention to the fact that this is a phenomenon which does not occur as a natural thing. This is indicated by the numerous laws which are necessary legally to guarantee this domination to men. It is also an indication that previous to the legal enforcement of masculine domination there must have been other epochs in which the masculine privilege was not nearly so certain. History proves that such epochs actually existed in the days of the matriarchate, the age in which it was the mother, the woman, who played the important rôle in life, particularly so far as the child was concerned. At that time each man in the clan was in duty bound to respect the honored position of the mother. Certain customs and usages are still colored by this ancient institution, as for instance, the introduction of all strange men to a child with the title of "uncle" or "cousin." A terrific battle must have preceded the transition from matriarchate to masculine domination. Men who like to believe that their privileges and prerogatives are determined by nature will be surprised to learn that men did not possess these prerogatives from the beginning, but had to fight for them.[1] The triumph of man was simultaneous with the subjugation of women, and it is especially the evidence in the development of the law which bears witness to this long process of subjugation.

Masculine dominance is not a natural thing. There is evidence to prove that it occurred chiefly as a result of constant battles between primitive peoples, during the course

[1] A very good description of this development can be found in August Bebel's "Woman and Socialism" and in Mathias and Mathilde Vaerting's "The Dominant Sex."

of which man assumed the more prominent rôle as warrior, and finally used his newly won superiority in order to retain the leadership for himself and for his own ends. Hand in hand with this development was a development of property rights and inheritance rights which became a basis of masculine domination, in so far as man usually was the acquirer and owner of property.

A growing child need not however read books on this theme. Despite the fact that he knows nothing of these archæological data he senses the fact that the male is the privileged member of the family. This occurs even when fathers and mothers with considerable insight are disposed to overlook those privileges which we have inherited from ancient days, in favor of a greater equality. It is very difficult to make it clear to a child that a mother who is engaged in household duties is as valuable as a father.

Think what it means to a young boy who sees the prevailing privilege of manhood before his eyes from his earliest days. From the day of his birth he is received with greater acclamation than a girl child. It is a well known and all too frequent occurrence that parents prefer to have boys as children. A boy senses at every step that, as a chip of the old block, he has certain privileges and a greater social value. Casual words directed toward him or taken up by him occasionally are constantly calling to his attention the fact of the greater importance of the masculine rôle.

The domination of the male also appears to him in the institution of female servants about the house who are used for menial tasks, and finally he is reinforced in his sentiments by the fact that the women in his environment are not at all convinced of their equality with men. That most important question which all women should ask their prospective husbands before marriage: "What is your attitude toward masculine domination, particularly in family life?" is usually never answered. In one case we find an expression of the striving for equality and in another case any of the various degrees of resignation. In contrast we see the father convinced from boyhood that as a man he has a more important rôle to play. He interprets this conviction as an implicit duty, and concerns himself solely with responding to the challenges of life and society in favor of masculine privilege.

Every situation which arises out of this relationship is experienced by the child. What he gets out of it is a number of pictures concerning the nature of woman, in which for the most part the woman plays a sorry figure. In this way the development of the boy has a distinct masculine color. What he believes to be the worth-while goals in his striving for power are exclusively masculine qualities and masculine attitudes. A typical masculine virtue grows out of these power relationships, which patently indicates its origins to us. Certain character traits count as masculine, others as feminine, albeit there is no basis to justify these valuations. If we compare the psychic state of boys and girls and seemingly find evidence in support of this classification, we do not deal with natural phenomena, but are describing the expressions of individuals who have been directed into a very specific channel, whose style of life and behavior pattern have been narrowed down by specific conceptions of power. These conceptions of power have indicated to them with compelling force the place where they must seek to develop. There is no justification for the differentiation of "manly" and "womanly" character traits. We shall see how both these traits are capable of being used to fulfill the striving for power. In other words, that one can express power with the so-called "feminine" traits, such as obedience and submission. The advantages which an obedient child enjoys can sometimes bring it much more into the lime-light than a disobedient child, though the striving for power is present in both cases. Our insight into psychic life is often made more difficult by the fact that striving for power expresses itself in the most complex fashion.

As a boy grows older his masculinity becomes a significant duty, his ambition, his desire for power and superiority is indisputably connected and identified with the duty to be masculine. For many children who desire power it is not sufficient to be simply aware of their masculinity; they must show a proof that they are men, and therefore they must have privileges. They accomplish this, on the one hand, by efforts to excel, thereby measuring their masculine traits; on the other hand they may succeed by tyrannizing their feminine environment in every possible way. According to the degree of resistance which they meet, these boys utilize either stubbornness and wild insurgency, or craft and cunning, to gain their ends.

Since every human being is measured according to the standard of the privileged male, it is no wonder that one always holds this standard before a boy. Finally he measures himself according to it, observing and asking whether his activities are sufficiently "masculine," whether he is "fully a man." What we consider "masculine" nowadays is common knowledge. Above all it is something purely egoistic, something which satisfies self-love, gives a feeling of superiority and domination over others, all with the aid of seemingly "active" characteristics such as courage, strength, duty, the winning of all manner of victories, especially those over women, the acquisition of positions, honors, titles, and the desire to harden himself against so-called "feminine" tendencies, and the like. There is a constant battle for personal superiority because it counts as a "masculine" virtue to be dominant.

In this manner every boy assumes characteristics which he sees in adult men, especially his father. We can trace the ramifications of this artificially nourished delusion of grandeur in the most diverse manifestations of our society. At an early age a boy is urged to secure for himself a reserve of power and privileges. This is what is called "manliness." In bad cases it degenerates into the well-known expressions of rudeness and brutality.

The advantages of being a man are, under such conditions, very alluring. We must not be astonished therefore when we see many girls who maintain a masculine ideal either as an unfulfilable desire, or as a standard for the judgment of their behavior; this ideal may evince itself as a pattern for action and appearance. It would seem that in our culture every woman wanted to be a man! In this class we find those girls particularly who have an uncontrollable desire to distinguish themselves in games and activities which are more appropriate to boys by virtue of their different physique. They climb up every tree, play rather with boys than with girls, and avoid every "womanly" activity as a shameful thing. Their satisfaction lies only in masculine activities. The preference for manliness makes all these phenomena understandable when we understand how the striving for superiority is more concerned with the symbols of things than with the activities of life.

III. The Alleged Inferiority of Women

Man has been wont to justify his domination not only by maintaining that his position is natural, but also that his dominance results from the inferiority of women. This conception of the inferiority of woman is so widespread that it appears as the common property of all races. Linked with this prejudice is a certain unrest on the part of men which may well have originated in the time of the war against the matriarchate, when woman was a source of actual anxiety. We come upon indications of this constantly in literature and history. A Latin author writes "Mulier est hominis confusio," "Woman is the confusion of man." In the theological consilia the question was often argued whether a woman had a soul, and learned theses were written concerning the question whether woman was actually a human being. The century-long period of witch-persecution and witch-burning is a sorry witness of the errors, the tremendous uncertainty and confusion of that happily forgotten age, concerning this question.

Woman was often held up as the source of all evil, as in the Biblical conception of the original sin, or as in the *Iliad* of Homer. The story of Helen demonstrated how one woman was capable of throwing whole peoples into misfortune. Legends and fairy tales of all times contain indices of the moral inferiority of woman, of her wickedness, of her falsity, of her treachery and of her fickleness. "Womanly folly" has even been used as an argument in legal cases. Coincident with these prejudices is the degradation of woman's capability, industry, and ability. Figures of speech, anecdotes, mottoes, and jokes, in all literatures and among all peoples, are full of degrading critiques of woman. Woman is reproached with her spitefulness, her pettiness, her stupidity, and the like.

An extraordinary acuity is sometimes developed in order to bear witness to the inferiority of woman. The number of men like Strindberg, Moebius, Schopenhauer, and Weininger, who have upheld this thesis, has been enlarged by a not inconsiderable number of women whose resignation has caused them to subscribe to a belief in the inferiority of woman. They are the champions of woman's rôle of submission. The degradation of woman and womanly labor is further indicated by the fact that women are paid less than men, regardless of whether their work is of equal value.

In the comparison of the results of intelligence and talent tests it was actually found that for particular subjects, as for instance, mathematics, boys showed more talent, whereas girls showed more talent for other subjects, such as languages. Boys actually do show greater talent than girls for studies which are capable of preparing them for their masculine occupation but this is only a seemingly greater talent. If we investigate the situation of the girls more closely we learn that the story of the lesser capability of woman is a palpable fable.

A girl is daily subjected to the argument that girls are less capable than boys and are suitable only for unessential activities. It is not surprising then that a girl is firmly convinced of the unchangeable and bitter fate of a woman and sooner or later because of her lack of training in childhood, actually believes in her own incapability. Discouraged in this manner, a girl approaches "masculine" occupations if the opportunity to approach them ever presents, with a foregone conclusion that she will not have the necessary interest for them. Should she possess such interest, she soon loses it, and thus she is denied both an outer and an inner preparation.

Under such circumstances proof of the incapability of woman seems valid. There are two causes for this. In the first place the error is accentuated by the fact that the value of a human being is frequently judged from purely business standpoints, or on one-sided and purely egoistic grounds. With such prejudices we can hardly be expected to understand how far performance and capability are coincident with psychic development. And this leads us to the second main factor to which the fallacy of the lesser capability of woman may thank its existence. It is a frequently overlooked fact that a girl comes into the world with a prejudice sounding in her ears which is designed only to rob her of her belief in her own value, to shatter her self-confidence and destroy her hope of ever doing anything worth while. If this prejudice is constantly being strengthened, if a girl sees again and again how women are given servile rôles to play, it is not hard to understand how she loses courage, fails to face her obligations, and sinks back from the solution of her life's problems. Then indeed she is useless and incapable! Yet if we approach a human being, undermine his self-respect so far as his relationship to society is concerned, cause him to abandon all hope of ever accomplishing anything, ruin his courage, and then find that he actually never amounts to anything, then we dare not maintain that we were right, for we must admit that it is *we* who have caused all his sorrow!

It is easy enough for a girl to lose her courage and her self-confidence in our civilization, yet, as a matter of fact, certain intelligence tests proved the interesting fact that in a certain group of girls, aged from 14 to 18, greater talent and capability were evinced than was shown by all other groups, boys included. Further researches show that these were all girls from families in which the mother was either the sole bread winner, or at least contributed largely to the family support. What this means is that these girls were in a situation at home in which the prejudice of the lesser capability of woman was either not present or existed only to a slight extent. They could see with their own eyes how their mothers' industry had its rewards, and as a result they developed themselves much more freely and much more independently, entirely uninfluenced by those inhibitions which are inevitably associated with the belief in the lesser powers of a woman.

A further argument against this prejudice is the not inconsiderable number of women who have accomplished results in the most varied fields, particularly in literature, art, crafts, and medicine, of such remarkable value that they are quite capable of standing any comparison with the results of men in these fields. There are so many men furthermore who not only do not show any achievements but are possessed of such a high grade of incapability that we could easily find an equal number of proofs (of course falsely) that men were the inferior sex.

One of the bitter consequences of the prejudice concerning the inferiority of women is the sharp division and pigeon-holing of concepts according to a scheme: thus "masculine" signifies worth-while, powerful, victorious, capable, whereas "feminine" becomes identical with obedient, servile, subordinate. This type of thinking has become so deeply anchored in human thought processes that in our civilization everything laudable has a "masculine" color whereas everything less valuable or actually derogatory is designated "feminine." We all know men who could not be more insulted than if we told them that they were feminine, whereas if we say to a girl that she is masculine it need signify no insult. The accent always falls so that everything which is reminiscent of woman appears inferior.

Character traits which would seem to prove this fallacious contention of the inferiority of woman prove themselves on closer observation nothing more than the manifestation of an inhibited psychic development. We do not maintain that we can make what is called a "talented" individual out of every child, but we can always make an "untalented" adult out of him. We have never done this fortunately. Others, however, we know have succeeded only too well. That such a fate overtakes girls more frequently than boys, in our day and age, is easily understood. We have often had the opportunity of seeing these "untalented" children suddenly become so talented that one might have spoken of a miracle!

IV. Desertion from Womanhood

The obvious advantages of being a man have caused severe disturbances in the psychic development of women as a consequence of which there is an almost universal dissatisfaction with the feminine rôle. The psychic life of woman moves in much the same channels, and under much the same rules, as that of any human beings who find themselves the possessors of a strong feeling of inferiority because of their situation in the scheme of things. The prejudice of her alleged inferiority as a woman signifies an additional aggravating complication. If a considerable number of girls find some sort of compensation, they owe it to their character development, to their intelligence, and sometimes to certain acquired privileges. This shows simply how one mistake may give rise to others. Such privileges are the special dispensations, exemptions from obligations, and the luxuries, which give a semblance of advantage in that they simulate what purports to be a high degree of respect for woman. There may be a certain degree of idealism in this, but finally this idealism is always an ideal which has been fashioned by men to the advantage of men. George Sand once described it very tellingly when she said: "The virtue of woman is a fine invention of man."

In general we can distinguish two types of women in the battle against the feminine rôle. One type has already been indicated: the girl who develops in an active, "masculine," direction. She becomes extraordinarily energetic and ambitious, and is constantly fighting for the prizes of life. She attempts to exceed her brothers and male comrades, chooses activities which are usually considered the privilege of men by preference, is interested in sports and the like. Very often she evades all the relationships of love and marriage. If she enters into such a relationship she may disturb its harmony by striving to be superior to her husband! She may have tremendous disinclination to any of the domestic activities. She may voice her disinclination directly, or indirectly by disavowing all talent for domestic duties, and constantly give evidence attempting to prove that she has never developed a talent for domesticity.

This is the type that seeks to compensate for the evil of the masculine attitude with a "masculine" response. The defense attitude toward womanhood is the foundation of her whole being. She has been designated "the boy-girl," "la garçonne," the "mannish" woman, and the like. This designation, however, is based upon a false conception.

There are many people who believe that there is a congenital factor present in such girls, a certain "masculine" substance or secretion which causes their "masculine" attitude. The whole history of civilization, however, shows us that the pressure exerted upon woman, and the inhibitions to which she must submit today, are not to be borne by any human being; they always give rise to revolt. If this revolt now exhibits itself in the direction which we call "masculine," the reason for it is simply that there are only *two* sex rôles possible. One must orient oneself according to one of two models, either that of an ideal woman, or according to that of an ideal man. Desertion from the rôle of woman can therefore appear only as "masculine," and vice versa. This does not occur as the result of some mysterious secretion, but because in the given time and place, there is no other possibility. We must never lose sight of the difficulties under which the psychic development of a girl takes place. So long as we cannot guarantee every woman an absolute equality with man we cannot demand her complete reconciliation with life, with the facts of our civilization, and the forms of our social life.

The woman who goes through life with an attitude of resignation, who exhibits an almost unbelievable degree of adjustment, obedience, and humbleness, belongs to the second type. Seemingly she adjusts herself everywhere, takes root wherever placed, but demonstrates such a high degree of clumsiness and helplessness that she accomplishes nothing at all! She may produce nervous symptoms, which serve her in her weakness, to demonstrate her need for consideration to others; and she shows clearly thereby how the training she has undergone, how her misuse of life, is regularly accompanied by nervous diseases, and makes her totally unfit for social life. She belongs to the best people in the world, but unfortunately she is sick and cannot meet the challenge of existence to any satisfying degree. She cannot win the satisfaction of her environment for any time. Her submission, her humility, her self-repression, is founded on the same revolt as that of her sister of the first type, a revolt which says clearly enough: "This is no happy life!"

The woman who does not defend herself against the womanly rôle but carries in herself the torturing consciousness that she is condemned to be an inferior being and ordained to play a subordinate rôle in life, makes up the third type. She is fully convinced of the inferiority of women, just as she is convinced that man alone is called upon to do the worth-while things in life. As a consequence, she approves his privileged position. Thus she swells the chorus of voices which sound the praises of man as the doer and the achiever, and demands a special position for him. She shows her feeling of weakness as clearly as if she wanted recognition for it, and demanded additional support because of it; but this attitude is the beginning of a long prepared revolt. By way of revenge she will shift her marital responsibilities upon her husband with a lighthearted catchword to the effect that "Only a man could do these things!"

Although woman is considered an inferior being, the business of education is largely delegated to her. Let us now picture these three types of woman for ourselves with reference to this most important and difficult task. At this juncture we can differentiate the types even more clearly. Women of the first type, the "masculine" attitude, will tyrannize, will occupy themselves with punishment, and thus exercise a tremendous pressure upon children, which these children will, of course, attempt to avoid. When this type of education is effective, its best possible result is a sort of military training which is quite valueless. Children usually think that mothers of this kind are very bad educators. The noise, the great to-do, always has a bad effect and there arises the danger that girls will be instigated to imitate them, whereas boys are frightened for the rest of their lives. Among men who have stood under the dominance of such mothers we shall find a number who avoid women as much as possible as though they had been inoculated with bitterness, and were incapable of bringing any sense of trust to a woman. What results is a definite division and separation between the sexes, whose pathology we can readily understand despite the fact that some investigators still exist who speak of a "faulty apportionment of the masculine and feminine elements."

Individuals of the other types are equally futile as educators. They may be so skeptical that the children soon discover their lack of self-confidence, and grow beyond them. In this case the mother renews her efforts, nags and scolds, and threatens to tell the father. The fact that she calls upon a masculine educator betrays her again, and shows her disbelief in the success of her educational activity. She deserts from the front in the matter of education just as though it were her duty to justify her standpoint that man alone is capable, and therefore, indispensable for education! Such women may simply avoid all educational efforts, and shift the responsibility therefor upon their husbands and governesses without compunction, since they feel they are incapable of any success.

Dissatisfaction with the womanly rôle is even more evident among girls who escape from life because of some so-called "higher" reasons. Nuns, or others who assume some occupation for which celibacy is an essential, are a case in point. Their lack of reconciliation with their rôle as women is clearly demonstrated in this gesture. Similarly, many girls go into business at an early age because the independence connected with employment seems a protection to them against the threatened necessity of marriage. Here again the driving power is the disinclination to assume the womanly rôle.

What of those cases in which marriage occurs, i one could believe that the rôle of woman ha tarily assumed? We learn that marriage need be an indication that a girl has reconciled herself with her womanly rôle. The example of a thirty-six-year-old woman is typical of this. She comes to the physician complaining of various nervous ills. She was the oldest child of a marriage between an aging man and a very domineering woman. The fact that her mother, a very beautiful young girl, had married an old man leads us to suspect that in the marriage of the parents the disinclination for the feminine rôle played some part. The marriage of the parents did not turn out happily. The mother ruled the house with clamor, and insisted upon having her will carried out at all costs, and regardless of anyone else's pleasure. The old man was forced into his corner at every opportunity. The daughter narrated how her mother would not even allow her father to lie down upon the sofa to rest. Her mother's whole activity consisted in maintaining certain "principles of domestic economy" which she felt were desirable to enforce. These were an absolute law to the family.

Our patient grew up a very capable child who was much pampered by the father. On the other hand, her mother was never satisfied with her and was always her enemy. Later, when a boy, toward whom the mother was far more favorable, was born, the relationship became unbearable. The little girl was conscious that she had a support in her father, who, no matter how modest and retiring he was in other things, could take up the cudgel when his daughter's interests were at stake. Thus she began to hate her mother cordially.

In this stubborn conflict the cleanliness of the mother became the daughter's favorite point of attack. The mother was so pedantic in her cleanliness that she did not even allow the servant girl to touch a door knob without wiping it off later. The child made it a point of special pleasure to ⁚o about as dirty and ill clad as possible, and to soil the ⸾use whenever the occasion offered.

⸾he developed all those characteristics which were the

exact opposite of that which her mother expected of her. This fact speaks very clearly against any inherited characteristics. If a child develops only those characteristics which must anger her mother almost to death, there is either a conscious or unconscious plan underlying them. The hate between mother and child has lasted until the present day, and a more bitter belligerency could not be imagined.

When this little girl was eight years old the following situation existed. The father was permanently on his daughter's side; her mother went about with a bitter face, making pointed remarks, enforcing her "rules," and reproaching the girl. The girl, embittered and belligerent, availed herself of an extraordinary sarcasm which crippled the activity of her mother. An additional complicating factor was the valvular heart disease of the younger brother who was his mother's favorite and a very much pampered child, who used his sickness to hold the attentions of his mother to an even more intensive degree. One could observe the constantly thwarted activities of the parents toward their children. Under such circumstances did this little girl grow up.

It then occurred that she fell sick of a nervous ailment which no one could explain. Her sickness consisted in the fact that she was tortured by evil thoughts which were directed against her mother, the consequence of which was that she felt herself hindered in all her activities. Finally she occupied herself very deeply, and suddenly, and without success, in religion. After some time these evil thoughts disappeared. Some medicine or other was given the credit for the disappearance, although it is more probable that her mother was forced into the defensive. A residue which expressed itself in a remarkable fear of thunder and lightning remained.

The little girl believed that the thunder and lightning came only as a result of her bad conscience, and would some day cause her death because she had such evil thoughts. One can see how the child was attempting to free herself of its

hate for its mother at this time. The development of the
child went further, and it seemed that a bright future was
beckoning her. The statement of a teacher who said: "This
little girl could do anything that she wanted to!" had a great
effect on her. These words are unimportant in themselves
but for this girl they meant, "I can accomplish something if
I wish." This realization was followed by an even greater
intensity in the combat against her mother.

Adolescence came, and she grew up into a beautiful
young woman, became marriageable, and had many suitors;
yet all opportunities of a relationship were broken off because of the peculiar sharpness of her tongue. She felt
herself drawn only to one man, an elderly man who lived in
her neighborhood, and everyone feared that some day she
might marry him. But this man moved after some time and
the girl remained, until she was twenty six years old, without a suitor. In the circles in which she moved this was very
remarkable, and no one could explain it because no one
understood her history. In the bitter battle which she had
been carrying on against her mother ever since her childhood, she had become unbearably quarrelsome. War was
her victory. The behavior of her mother had constantly
irritated this child and caused her to seek for fresh triumphs.
A bitter word-battle was her greatest happiness; in this she
showed her vanity. Her "masculine" attitude expressed itself
also in that she desired such word battles only where she
could conquer her opponent.

When she was twenty-six years old she made the acquaintance of a very honorable man who did not allow himself to
be repulsed by her belligerent character and paid court to
her very earnestly. He was very humble and submissive in
his approach. Pressure from her relatives to marry this man
led her to explain repeatedly that he was so very unpleasant
to her that she could not think of marriage with him. This
is not hard to understand when we know her character, yet
after two years of resistance she finally accepted him in the

deep conviction that she had made a slave of him, and that she could do with this man whatever she wished. She had hoped secretly that she would find in him a second edition of her father, who would give in to her whenever she wanted.

She soon learned that she had made a mistake. A few days after her marriage her husband was sitting in the room smoking his pipe and comfortably reading his paper. In the morning he left for his office, came home punctually for his meals, and grumbled a little if his meals were not ready. He demanded cleanliness, tenderness, punctuality, and all manner of unjustified requests which she was not prepared to fulfil. The relationship was not even remotely similar to that which she had experienced between herself and her father. She tumbled out of all her dreams. The more she demanded, the less her husband acceded to her wishes, and the more he indicated her domestic rôle to her, the less he saw of her domestic activity. She did not lose the opportunity to remind him daily that he really had no right to make these requests, as she had expressly told him that she did not like him. This made absolutely no impression upon him. He continued his demands with an inexorableness which caused her to have very unhappy prospects for the future. In an intoxication of self-effacement this righteous, dutiful man had wooed her, but no sooner did he have her in his possession, than his intoxication had disappeared.

No change in the lack of harmony which existed between them appeared when she became a mother. She was forced to assume new duties. In the meantime her relationship to her own mother, who was energetically taking up the cudgels for her son-in-law, became worse and worse. The constant warfare in her house was carried on with such heavy artillery that it is not to be wondered that her husband occasionally acted badly, and without consideration, and that occasionally the woman was right in her complaints. The behavior of her husband was the direct consequence of the fact that she was unapproachable, which, again, was a result of her lack of reconciliation with her womanliness. She had believed originally that she could play her rôle of empress forever, that she could wander through life surrounded by a slave who would carry out all her wishes. Life would have been possible for her only under these circumstances.

What could she do now? Should she divorce her husband and return to her mother and declare herself beaten? She was incapable of leading an independent life for she had never been prepared for it. A divorce would have been an insult to her pride and vanity. Life was misery for her; on the one hand her husband criticised her, and on the other side stood her mother with her heavy guns, preaching cleanliness and order.

Suddenly she, too, became cleanly and orderly! She did washing and polishing and cleaning the whole day. It seemed as though she had finally seen the light, and had acquired the teachings which her mother had drummed into her ears for so many years. In the beginning her mother must have smiled, and her husband must have been pleased at this sudden change of affairs, at the sight of this young woman emptying and cleaning bureaus, cabinets, and closets. But one can carry a thing like this too far. She washed and scoured so long, until there was not an unscrubbed shred in the house, and her zeal was so apparent that she was disturbed by everyone in her efforts; and in turn disturbed everyone else in her zeal. If she washed something and another touched it, then she would have to wash it again, and only she could do it.

The disease which manifests itself in continual washing and cleaning is an extraordinarily frequent occurrence in women who are belligerent against their womanliness and attempt in this fashion to elevate themselves by their complete virtue in cleanliness, over those who do not wash themselves so frequently. Unconsciously all these efforts are aimed solely at exploding the entire household. Few households were ever more disorderly than the household of this woman. Not cleanliness, but the discomfiture of her entire household, was her goal.

We could tell of very many cases in which a reconciliation with the rôle of being a woman was only *apparently* true. That our patient had no friends among women, could get along with no one, and knew no consideration for another human being, fits very well into the pattern which we might have expected in her life.

It will be necessary for us to evolve better methods of educating girls in the future, so that they shall be better prepared to reconcile themselves with life. Under the most favorable circumstances it is occasionally impossible to effect this reconciliation with life, as in this case. The alleged inferiority of woman is maintained in our age by law and tradition, though it is denied by anyone with a real psychological insight. We must therefore be on the watch to recognize and counter the whole technique of society's mistaken behavior in this connection. We must take up the battle not because we have some pathologically exaggerated respect for woman, but because the present fallacious attitude negates the logic of our whole social life.

Let us take this occasion to discuss another relationship which is often used in order to degrade woman: the so-called "dangerous age," that period which occurs about the fiftieth year, accompanied by the accentuation of certain character traits. Physical changes serve to indicate to woman in the menopause that the bitter time in which she must lose forever that little semblance of significance which she has so laboriously built up during the course of her life, has come. Under these circumstances she searches with redoubled efforts for any instrument which will be useful in maintaining her position, now grown more precarious than ever before. Our civilization is dominated by a principle in which present performance alone is a source of value; every aging individual, but especially a woman who is growing

old, experiences difficulties at this time. The damage which
is done to an aging woman by entirely undermining her
value affects every human being, in so far as we cannot
count our worth solely from day to day in the prime of life.
What one has accomplished at the height of his activities
must be credited to him during the years in which his powers
and activity are of necessity lessened. It is not right to exclude someone entirely from the spiritual and material relationships of society simply because he is growing old. In
the case of a woman this amounts to a virtual degradation
and enslavement. Imagine the anxiety of an adolescent girl
who thinks of this epoch in her life which lies in her future.
Womanliness is not extinguished with the fiftieth year. The
honor and worth of a human being lasts unaltered beyond
this age. And it must be guaranteed.

V. Tension between the Sexes

The foundations of all these unhappy manifestations are
built upon the mistakes of our civilization. If our civilization is marked by a prejudice, then this prejudice reaches
out and touches every aspect of that civilization, and is to
be found in its every manifestation. The fallacy of the inferiority of woman, and its corollary, the superiority of
man, constantly disturbs the harmony of the sexes. As a
result, an unusual tension is introduced into all erotic relationships, thereby threatening, and often entirely annihilating, every chance for happiness between the sexes. Our
whole love life is poisoned, distorted, and corroded by this
tension. This explains why one so seldom finds a harmoni-
ous marriage, this is the reason so many children grow up
in the feeling that marriage is something extremely difficult
and dangerous.

Prejudices such as we have described above prevent children, to a large measure, from understanding life ade-

quately. Think of the numerous young girls who consider marriage only as a sort of emergency exit out of life, and think of those men and women who see in marriage only a necessary evil! The difficulties which originally grew out of this tension between the sexes have assumed gigantic proportions today. They become greater and greater the more clearly a girl acquires the tendency to avoid the sexual rôle which society compels her to assume and the more, in the case of a man, there is a desire to play the privileged rôle despite all the false logic in such behavior.

Comradeship is the characteristic index of a true reconciliation with the sexual rôle, of a veritable equilibrium between the sexes. A subordination of one individual to another in sexual relationships is just as unbearable as in the life of nations. Everyone should consider this problem very attentively since the difficulties which may arise for each partner from a mistaken attitude are considerable. This is an aspect of our life which is so widespread and important that every one of us is involved in it. It becomes the more complicated since in our day a child is forced into a behavior pattern which is a depreciation and negation of the other sex.

A calm education certainly could overcome these difficulties, but the hurry of our days, the lack of really proved and tested educational methods, and particularly the competitive nature of our whole life which reaches even into the nursery, determine only too harshly the tendencies of later life. The fear which causes so many human beings to shrink from assuming any love relationships is caused largely by the useless pressure which forces every man to prove his masculinity under all circumstances, even though he must do it by treachery and malice or force.

That this serves to destroy all candor and trust in the love relationships is self-understood. The Don Juan is a man who doubts his own manliness, and is seeking constant additional evidence for it, in his conquests. The distrust which is so universal between the sexes prevents all frankness, and humanity as a whole suffers as a consequence. The exaggerated masculine ideal signifies a constant challenge, a constant spur, a restlessness whose results naturally are only vanity and self enrichment, maintenance of the "privileged" attitude; and all these of course, are contrary to a healthy communal life. We have no reason to combat the former purposes of the emancipation-for-women movements. It is our duty to support them in their efforts to gain freedom and equality, because finally the happiness of the whole of humanity depends upon effecting such conditions that a woman will be enabled to be reconciled with her womanly rôle, just as the possibility of a man's adequate solution of his relationship to woman likewise depends upon it.

VI. Attempts at Reform

Of all the institutions which have been developed to better the relationship between the sexes, co-education is the most important. This institution is not universally accepted; it has its opponents, and its friends. Its friends maintain as their most powerful argument that, through co-education, the two sexes have an opportunity to become acquainted with one another at an early date and that through this acquaintanceship the fallacious prejudices, and their disastrous consequences, can be prevented in a measure. The opponents usually counter that boys and girls are already so different at the time that they enter school that their co-education results only in accentuating these differences, because the boys feel themselves under pressure. This occurs because the spiritual development of girls advances more quickly than that of boys during the school years. These boys, under the necessity of carrying their privilege and giving evidence of the fact that they are more capable, must suddenly recognize that their privilege is only a soap bubble which in reality bursts very easily. Other investigators have maintained that in co-education boys become anxious in front of girls, and lose their self-esteem.

There is no doubt that some measure of truth lies in these arguments, but they hold water only when we consider co-education in the sense of *competition* between the sexes, for the prize of greater talent and capability. If that is what co-education means to teachers and pupils, it is a damaging doctrine. If we cannot find any teachers who have a better notion of co-education, that is, that it represents a training and preparation for future *cooperation* between the sexes in communal tasks, then every attempt at co-education must fail. Its opponents will see but an affirmation of their attitude in its failure.

It would require the creative power of a poet to give an adequate picture of this whole situation. We must be content to indicate only the main points. An adolescent girl acts very much as though she were inferior, and what we have said concerning the compensation of organic inferiorities holds equally well for her. The difference is this: the belief in her inferiority is forced upon a girl by her environment. She is so irrevocably guided into this channel of behavior that even investigators with a great deal of insight have from time to time fallen into the fallacy of believing in her inferiority. The universal result of this fallacy is that both sexes have finally fallen into the hasty pudding of prestige politics, and each tries to play a rôle for which he is not suited. What happens? Both their lives become complicated, their relationships are robbed of all candor, they become surfeited with fallacies and prejudices, in the face of which all hope of happiness vanishes.

CHAPTER VIII

THE FAMILY CONSTELLATION

We have often drawn attention to the fact that before we can judge a human being we must know the situation in which he grew up. An important moment is the position which a child occupied in his family constellation. Frequently we can catalogue human beings according to this view point after we have gained sufficient expertness, and can recognize whether an individual is a first-born, an only child, the youngest child, or the like.

People seem to have known for a long time that the youngest child is usually a peculiar type. This is evidenced by the countless fairy tales, legends, Biblical stories, in which the youngest always appears in the same light. As a matter of fact he does grow up in a situation quite different from that of all other people, for to parents he represents a particular child, and as the youngest he experiences an especially solicitous treatment. Not only is he the youngest, but also usually the smallest, and by consequence, the most in need of help. His other brothers and sisters have already acquired some degree of independence and growth during the time of his weakness, and for this reason he usually grows up in an atmosphere warmer than that which the others have experienced.

Hence there arise a number of characteristics which influence his attitude toward life in a remarkable way, and cause him to be a remarkable personality. One circumstance which seemingly is a contradiction for our theory must be noted. No child likes to be the smallest, the one whom one does not trust, the one in whom one has no confidence, all the time. Such knowledge stimulates a child to prove that he can do everything. His striving for power becomes markedly accentuated and we find the youngest very usually a man who has developed a desire to overcome all others, satisfied only with the very best.

This type is not uncommon. One group of these youngest children excels every other member of the family, and becomes the family's most capable member. But there is another more unfortunate group of these same youngest children; they also have a desire to excel, but lack the necessary activity and self-confidence, as a result of their relationships to their older brothers and sisters. If the older children are not to be excelled, the youngest frequently shies from his tasks, becomes cowardly, a chronic plaintiff forever seeking an excuse to evade his duties. He does not become less ambitious, but he assumes that type of ambition which forces him to wriggle out of situations, and satisfy his ambition in activity outside of the necessary problems of life, to the end that he may avoid the danger of an actual test of ability, so far as possible.

It will undoubtedly have occurred to many readers that the youngest child acts as though he were neglected and carried a feeling of inferiority within him. In our investigations we have always been able to find this feeling of inferiority and have been able also to deduce the quality and fashion of his psychic development from the presence of this torturing sentiment. In this sense a youngest child is like a child who has come into the world with weak organs. What the child *feels* need not actually be the case. It does not matter what really has happened, whether an individual is really inferior or not. What is important is his *interpretation* of his situation. We know very well that mistakes are easily made in childhood. At that time a child is faced with a great number of questions, of possibilities, and consequences.

What shall an educator do? Shall he impose additional

stimuli by spurring on the vanity of this child? Should he constantly push him into the limelight so that he is always the first? This would be a feeble response to the challenge of life. Experience teaches us that it makes very little difference whether one is first or not. It would be better to exaggerate in the other direction, and maintain that being first, or the best, is unimportant. We are really tired of having nothing but the first and best people. History as well as experience demonstrates that happiness does not consist in being the first or best. To teach a child such a principle makes him one-sided; above all it robs him of his chance of being a good fellow-man.

The first consequence of such doctrines is that a child thinks only of himself and occupies himself in wondering whether someone will overtake him. Envy and hate of his fellows and anxiety for his own position, develop in his soul. His very place in life makes a speeder trying to beat out all others, of the youngest. The racer, the marathon runner in his soul, is betrayed by his whole behavior, especially in little gestures which are not obvious to those who have not learned to judge his psychic life in all his relationships. These are the children, for instance, who always march at the head of the procession and cannot bear to have anyone in front of them. Some such race-course attitude is characteristic of a large number of children.

This type of the youngest child is occasionally to be found as a clear cut type example although variations are common. Among the youngest we find active and capable individuals who have gone so far that they have become the saviors of their whole family. Consider the Biblical story of Joseph! Here is a wonderful exposition of the situation of the youngest son. It is as though the past had told us about it with a purpose and a clarity arising in the full possession of the evidence which we acquire so laboriously today. In the course of the centuries much valuable material has been lost which we must attempt to find again.

Another type, which grows secondarily from the first, is often found. Consider our marathon runner who suddenly comes to an obstacle which he does not trust himself to hurdle. He attempts to avoid the difficulty by going around it. When a youngest child of this type loses his courage he becomes the most arrant coward that we can well imagine. We find him far from the front, every labor seems too much for him, and he becomes a veritable "alibi artist" who attempts nothing useful, but spends his whole energy wasting time. In any actual conflict he always fails. Usually he is to be found carefully seeking a field of activity in which every chance of competition has been excluded. He will always find excuses for his failures. He may contend that he was too weak or petted, or that his brothers and sisters did not allow him to develop. His fate becomes more bitter if he actually has a physical defect, in which case he is certain to make capital out of his weakness to justify him in his desertion.

Both these types are hardly ever good fellow human beings. The first type fares better in a world where competition is valued for itself. A man of this type will maintain his spiritual equilibrium only at the cost of others, whereas individuals of the second remain under the oppressive feeling of their inferiority and suffer from their lack of reconciliation with life as long as they live.

The oldest child also has well defined characteristics. For one thing he has the advantage of an excellent position for the development of his psychic life. History recognizes that the oldest son has had a particularly favorable position. Among many peoples, in many classes, this advantageous status has become traditional. There is no question for instance that among the European farmers the first born knows his position from his early childhood and realizes that some day he will take over the farm, and therefore he finds himself in a much better position than the other children who know that they must leave their father's farm at some time; in other strata of society it is frequently held that the oldest son will some day be the head of the house. Even where this tradition has not actually become crystallized, as in simple bourgeois or proletarian families, the oldest child is usually the one whom one accredits with enough power and common sense to be the helper or foreman of his parents. One can imagine how valuable it is to a child to be constantly entrusted with responsibilities by his environment. We can imagine that his thought processes are somewhat like this: "You are the larger, the stronger, the older, and therefore you must also be cleverer than the others."

If his development in this direction goes on without disturbance then we shall find him with the traits of a guardian of law and order. Such persons have an especially high evaluation of power. This extends not only to their own personal power, but affects their evaluation of the concepts of power in general. Power is something which is quite self-understood for the oldest child, something which has weight and must be honored. It is not surprising that such individuals are markedly conservative.

The striving for power in the case of a second born child also has its especial nuance. Second born children are constantly under steam, striving for superiority under pressure: the race course attitude which determines their activity in life is very evident in their actions. The fact that there is someone ahead of him who has already gained power is a strong stimulus for the second born. If he is enabled to develop his powers and takes up the battle with the first born he will usually move forward with a great deal of élan, the while the first born, possessing power, feels himself relatively secure until the second threatens to surpass him.

This situation has also been described in a very lively fashion in the Biblical legend of Esau and Jacob. In this story the battle goes on relentlessly, not so much for actual power, but for the semblance of power; in cases like this it continues with a certain compulsion until the goal is reached and the first born is overcome, or the battle is lost, and the retreat, which often evinces itself in nervous diseases, begins. The attitude of the second born is similar to the envy of the poor classes. There is a dominant note of being slighted, neglected, in it. The second born may place his goal so high that he suffers from it his whole life, annihilates his inner harmony in following, not the veritable facts of life, but an evanescent fiction and the valueless semblance of things.

The only child of course finds himself in a very particular situation. He is at the utter mercy of the educational methods of his environment. His parents, so to speak, have no choice in the matter. They place their whole educational zeal upon their only child. He becomes dependent to a high degree, waits constantly for someone to show him the way, and searches for support at all times. Pampered throughout his life, he is accustomed to no difficulties, because one has always removed difficulties from his way. Being constantly the center of attention he very easily acquires the feeling that he really counts for something of great value. His position is so difficult that mistaken attitudes are almost inevitable in his case. If the parents understand the dangers of his situation, to be sure, there is a possibility of preventing many of them, but at best it remains a difficult problem.

Parents of "only" children are frequently exceptionally cautious, people who have themselves experienced life as a great danger, and therefore approach their child with an inordinate solicitude. The child in turn interprets their attentions and admonitions as a source of additional pressure. Constant attention to health and well being finally stimulate him to conceive of the world as a very hostile place. An eternal fear of difficulties arises in him and he approaches them in an unpractised and clumsy manner because he has tested only the pleasant things in life. Such children have difficulties with every independent activity and sooner or later they become useless for life. Shipwrecks in their life's activity are to be expected. Their life approaches that of a parasite who does nothing, but enjoys life while the rest of the world cares for his wants.

Various combinations are possible in which several brothers and sisters of the same or opposite sexes compete with each other. The evaluation of any one case therefore becomes exceedingly difficult. The situation of an only boy among several girls is a case in point. A feminine influence dominates such a household and the boy is pushed into the background, particularly if he is the youngest, and sees himself opposed by a closed phalanx of women. His striving for recognition encounters great difficulties. Threatened on all sides, he never senses with certainty the privilege which in our retarded masculine civilization is given to every male. A lasting insecurity, an inability to evaluate himself as a human being, is his most characteristic trait. He may become so intimidated by his womenfolk that he feels that to be a man is equivalent to occupying a position of lesser honor. On the one hand his courage and self-confidence may easily be eclipsed, or on the other the stimulus may be so drastic that the young boy forces himself to great achievements. Both cases arise from the same situation. What becomes of such boys in the end is determined by other concomitant and closely related phenomena.

We see therefore that the very position of the child in the family may lend shape and color to all the instincts, tropisms, faculties and the like, which he brings with him into the world. This affirmation robs of all value the theories of the inheritance of especial traits or talents, which are so harmful to all educational effort. There are doubtless occasions and cases in which the effect of hereditary influences can be shown, as for instance, in a child who grows up removed entirely from his parents, yet develops certain similar "familial" traits. This becomes much more comprehensible if one remembers how closely certain types of mistaken development in a child are related to inherited defects of the body. Take a given child who comes into the world with a weak body which results, in turn, in his greater tension toward the demands of life and his environment. If his father came into the world with similarly defective organs and approached the world with a similar tension, it is not to be wondered at that similar mistakes and character traits should result. Viewed from this standpoint it would seem to us that the theory of inheritance of acquired characteristics is based upon very weak evidence.

From our previous descriptions we may assume that whatever the errors to which a child is exposed in his development, the most serious consequences arise from his desire to elevate himself over all his fellows, to seek more personal power which will give him advantages over his fellow man. In our culture he is practically compelled to develop according to a fixed pattern. If we wish to prevent such a pernicious development we must know the difficulties he has to meet and understand them. There is one single and essential point of view which helps us to overcome all these difficulties; it is the view-point of the development of the social feeling. If this development succeeds, obstacles are insignificant, but since the opportunities for this development are relatively rare in our culture, the difficulties which a child encounters play an important rôle. Once this is recognized we shall not be surprised to find many people who spend their whole life fighting for their lives and others to whom life is a vale of sorrows. We must understand that they are the victims of a mistaken development whose unfortunate consequence is that their attitude toward life also is mistaken.

Let us be very modest then, in our judgment of our fellows, and above all, let us never allow ourselves to make any *moral* judgments, judgments concerning the moral worth of a human being! On the contrary we must make our knowledge of these facts socially valuable. We must approach such a mistaken and misled human being sympathetically, because we are in a position to have a much better idea of what is going on within him than he is himself. This gives rise to important new points of view in the matter of education. The very recognition of the source of error puts a great many influential instruments for betterment into our hands. By analysing the psychic structure and development of any human being we understand not only his past, but may deduce further what his future probably will be. Thus our science gives us some conception of what a human being really is. He becomes a living being for us, not merely a flat silhouette. And as a consequence we can have a richer and more meaningful sense of his value as a fellow human than is usual in our day.

BOOK II

THE SCIENCE OF CHARACTER

CHAPTER I

GENERAL CONSIDERATIONS

I. The Nature and Origin of Character

What we call a character trait is the appearance of some specific mode of expression on the part of an individual who is attempting to adjust himself to the world in which he lives. Character is a social concept. We can speak of a character trait only when we consider the relationship of an individual to his environment. It would make very little difference what kind of character Robinson Crusoe had. Character is a psychic attitude, it is the quality and nature of an individual's approach to the environment in which he moves. It is the behavior pattern according to which his striving for significance is elaborated in the terms of his social feeling.

We have already seen how the goal of superiority, of power, of the conquest of others, is the goal which directs the activity of most human beings. This goal modifies the world philosophy and the behavior pattern and directs the various psychic expressions of an individual into specific channels. Traits of character are only the external manifestations of the style of life, of the behavior pattern, of any individual. As such they enable us to understand his attitude towards his environment, towards his fellow men, towards the society in which he lives, and towards the challenge of existence in general. Character traits are instruments, the tricks which are used by the total personality in the acquisition of recognition and significance; their configuration in the personality amounts to a "technique" in living.

Traits of character are not inherited, as many would

have it, nor are they congenitally present. They are to be considered as similar to a pattern for existence which enables every human being to live his life and express his personality in any situation without the necessity of consciously thinking about it. Character traits are not the expressions of inherited powers nor predispositions but they are acquired for the purpose of maintaining a particular habitus in life. A child, for instance, is not born lazy but is lazy because laziness seems to him the best adapted means of making life easier, while it enables him at the same time to maintain his feeling of significance. The power attitude can be expressed in a certain degree, in the pattern of laziness. An individual may draw attention to a congenital defect and thus save his face before a defeat. The end result of such introspection is always something like this: 'If I did not have this defect my talents would develop brilliantly. But unfortunately I *have* the defect!" A second individual who is involved in a long-standing war with his environment because of his undisciplined striving for power, will develop whatever power expressions are adequate to his battle, such as ambition, envy, mistrust, and the like. We believe that such traits of character are indistinguishable from the personality, but are not inherited nor unchangeable. Closer observation shows us that they have been found necessary and adequate for the behavior pattern and have been acquired to this end, sometimes very early in life. They are not primary factors, but secondary ones, which have been forced into being by the secret goal of the personality.

Every child is faced with so many obstacles in life that no child ever grows up without striving for some form of significance. The form which this striving will take is interchangeable, and every human being approaches the problem of his personal significance in an individual way. The assertion that children are similar to their parents in their character traits, is easily explained by the fact that the child, in his striving for significance, seizes upon the example of those individuals in his environment who are already significant and demand respect, as an ideal model. Every generation learns from its ancestors in this way, and it maintains what it has learned in the greatest difficulties and complexities to which this striving for power may lead it.

The goal of superiority is a secret goal. The existence of a social feeling prevents its frank development. It must grow in secret and hide itself behind a friendly mask! We must reaffirm however that it would not grow with such tropic luxuriance if we humans understood one another better. If we could go so far that each of us developed better eyes and could more transparently view the character of his neighbor, then we should not only be able to protect ourselves better, but simultaneously make it so difficult for another to express his striving for power, that it would not pay him to do so. Under such circumstances the veiled striving for power would disappear. It pays us therefore to look into these relationships more closely and make use of the experimental evidence which we have won.

II. The Significance of the Social Feeling for the Development of Character

The social feeling, next to the striving for power, plays the most important rôle in the development of character. It is expressed, just as is the striving for significance, in the first psychic tendencies of the child, especially in his desire for contact and tenderness. We have already learned about the conditions for the development of the social feeling in a previous paragraph, and we wish merely to recall them briefly. The social feeling is influenced both by the feeling of inferiority and its compensatory striving for power. Human beings are very sensitive media for the development of inferiority complexes of all kinds. The process of psychic life, the disquiet that seeks for compensations, that demands security and totality, begins as soon as the feeling of inferiority appears, for the purpose of securing peace and happiness in life. The rules of conduct which we must maintain toward a child grow out of our recognition of his feeling of inferiority. These rules may be summed up with the admonition that we must not make life too bitter for a child, and that we must prevent him from learning the dark side of existence too quickly; and that we must also give him the possibility of experiencing the joy of living. A second group of conditions, which are of an economic nature, comes into play here. Unfortunately, children often grow up in circumstances which are unnecessarily bitter; misunderstanding, poverty, and want, are phenomena which may be prevented. Bodily defects play an important rôle because they can cause a normal style of life to be impossible and teach a child that he needs special privileges and particular laws in order to maintain his existence. Even if we had all these things in our power, we could not prevent the fact that such children would experience life as an unpleasant difficulty and this in turn gives rise to the great danger that their social feeling will become distorted.

We cannot judge a human being except by using the concept of the social feeling as a standard, and measuring his thought and action according to it. We must maintain this standpoint, because every individual within the body of human society must affirm the connectedness of that society. The necessity causes us to recognize more or less clearly, what we owe our fellow-men. We are in the very midst of life and are dominated by the logic of communal existence. This determines the fact that we need certain known criteria for the evaluation of our fellows. The degree to which the social feeling has developed in any individual is the sole criterion of human values, universally valid. We cannot deny our psychic dependency upon the social feeling. There is no human being who is capable of actually breaking off his social feeling in its entirety. There are no words with which we could entirely escape our duties to our fellow-man. The social feeling constantly reminds us with its warning voice. This does not mean that we constantly have the social feeling in our conscious thought, but we do maintain that a certain mobilization of power is required to distort it, to set it aside; and further, its universal necessity permits no one to begin an action without first being justified by this social feeling. The need for justifying each act and thought originates in the unconscious sense of social unity. At the very least it determines the fact that we frequently must seek extenuating circumstances for our actions. Herein originates the special technique of life, of thinking and acting, which causes us to wish to remain constantly in rapport with the social feeling, or at the very least, to delude ourselves with the semblance of social connectedness. In short, these explanations show that there is something like a mirage of the social feeling, which acts as a veil cloaking certain tendencies. The discovery of these tendencies alone would give us a correct evaluation of an action or an individual. That such deception may occur, increases the difficulty in evaluating the social feeling; it is this very difficulty which raises the understanding of human nature to the plane of a science.

There is an anecdote which may well serve to show the difference between true and false social feeling. An old lady while attempting to board a street car, slipped and fell into the snow. She could not arise, and a number of people hurried past her without noticing her plight, until a man stepped to her side, and helped her up. At this moment another man, who had been hidden somewhere, jumped to her side and greeted her chivalrous savior with these words: "Thank God! I have finally found a decent man. I have been standing here for five minutes, waiting to see whether someone would help the old lady up. You are the first one to do it!" This incident shows how the semblance of a social feeling may be misused. By this palpable trick one man has set himself up as a judge of others, distributes praise and blame, but has not lifted a finger himself to help a situation of which he was a witness.

There are other more complicated cases in which it is not easy to decide how great or how little the social feeling is. Nothing remains but to investigate them radically. Once this is done we do not long remain in the dark. There is the case, for instance, of a General who, although he knew a battle already half lost, forced thousands of soldiers to die unnecessarily. This General certainly said he was acting in the interests of the nation, and many people agreed with him. Yet it would be difficult to consider him a real fellow man, whatever reasons he may have brought to justify himself.

In these uncertain cases we need a standpoint which is universally applicable in order to judge correctly. For us such a standpoint can be found in the concept of social usefulness and the general well-being of humanity, the "common weal." If we assume this standpoint we shall only very rarely have difficulty in deciding a particular case.

The degree of the social feeling shows itself in an individual's every activity. It may be very obvious in his external expressions, as, for instance, the way he looks at another person, his manner of shaking hands, or of speaking. His whole personality may give an indelible impression, one way or another, which we sense almost intuitively. Occasionally we draw such far-reaching conclusions unconsciously from the behavior of a man, that our own attitude is quite dependent upon them. In these discussions we are doing little else than bringing this intuitive knowledge into the sphere of consciousness, and thus enabling ourselves to test and evaluate it, to the end that we may avoid making great mistakes. The value of this transference into consciousness lies in that we lay ourselves less open to false prejudices (which are active when we allow our judgments to be formed in the unconscious where we cannot control our activities and have no opportunity to make revisions).

Let us reaffirm that an evaluation of a man's character must be made solely when his context, his environment, is known. If we wrench single phenomena from his life and judge them singly, as one might if one considered his physical status alone, or solely his environment, or education, we are inevitably forced into erroneous conclusions. This thesis is valuable because it immediately removes a great load from the shoulders of mankind. A better knowledge of ourselves must, with our technique of living, result in a behavior pattern more appropriate to our needs. It becomes possible by applying our method, to influence others, especially children, for the better, and prevent the inexorable consequences of the blind fate which might otherwise overtake them. Thus it will no longer be necessary for an individual to be condemned to an unhappy fate simply because he originated in an unfortunate family, or hereditary, situation. Let us accomplish this alone, and our civilization will have taken a decided step in advance! A new generation will grow up courageously conscious that it is master of its own fate!

III. The Direction of Character Development

Any character traits which are conspicuous in a personality must be appropriate to the direction which his psychic development has taken from childhood. This direction may be a straight line or it may be marked by shunts and détours. In the first instance, a child strives for the realization of his goal along a direct line, and develops an aggressive, courageous character. The beginnings of character development usually are marked by such active, aggressive, traits. But this line is easily diverted or modified. Difficulties may be inherent in the greater resistive powers of the child's opponents, who prevent the child from gaining his goal of superiority by straight-forward attack. The child will attempt in some way to circumvent these difficulties. His detour, again, will determine specific character traits. Other difficulties in development of the character, such as the deficient development of organs, repulses and defeats at the hands of his environment, have a similar effect upon him. Further, the influence of that greater environment, the world, the teacher who cannot be avoided, is of great importance. The business of living in our civilization, as expressed in the demands, doubts, and emotions of a child's teachers, ultimately affects his character. All education takes on the color and the attitude best calculated to develop a pupil in the direction of the social life and the prevailing culture of his times.

Obstacles of every sort are dangerous for a straight-line development of character. Where they are present, the paths by which a child will seek to accomplish his goal of power will deviate to a greater or lesser degree from the straight line. In the first case the attitude of the child will be undisturbed, and he will approach his difficulties directly, whereas in the second case we have the picture of an entirely different child, a child who has learned that fire burns, that there are opponents in whose presence one must be careful. He will attempt to attain his goal of recognition and power along psychic détours, not directly, but by craft. His development is relative to the degree of such deviations. Whether or not he is over-cautious, whether or not he finds himself in tune with the necessities of life, or whether or not he has avoided these necessities, will depend upon the afore-mentioned factors. If he will not approach his tasks and problems directly, if he becomes cowardly and timid, refuses to look another straight in the eye, or to speak the truth, it is solely another type of child: his goal is identical with that of the courageous child. If two people act differently, their goal may nevertheless be the same!

Both types of character development may exist to a certain degree in the same individual. This occurs especially when the child has not crystallized his trends too sharply, when his principles are still elastic, when he does not always assume the same path, but retains sufficient initiative to look for another approach if the first attempt proves inadequate.

An undisturbed communal social life is the first premise for an adaptation to the demands of the community. One can easily teach a child this adaptation so long as he is not in a belligerent attitude toward his environment. War within the family may be eliminated only when the educators are capable of minimizing their own striving for power to such a degree that it does not act as a burden upon a child. If in addition, the parents understand the principles of a child's development, they can avoid the development of straight line character traits into their exaggerated forms, as the degeneration of courage into impudence, of independence into raw egoism. Similarly they will be able to avoid any external, forcibly produced authority, from producing signs of servile obedience. Pernicious training of this sort may otherwise cause the child to be shut in, afraid of the truth, and the consequences of frankness. Pressure, when used in education, is a double-edged sword. It produces the semblance of adaptation. Compulsive obedience is only apparent obedience. The reflection of the general relationships of the child to his environment is to be found in his soul. Whether all the conceivable obstacles which may be present act directly or indirectly upon him will also be reflected in his personality. A child is usually incapable of exercising any critique of outside influences; and his adult environment either knows nothing of them or cannot understand them. The constellation of his difficulties, plus his reaction to his obstacles, constitutes his personality.

There is another scheme according to which we can catalogue human beings. The criterion is the manner in

which they approach difficulties. In the first place there are
the optimists, who are individuals whose character development, by and large, has been in a direct line. They approach
all difficulties courageously and do not take them too seriously. They maintain their belief in themselves and assume
a happy attitude toward life with comparative ease. They
do not demand too much of life because they have a good
evaluation of themselves, and do not consider themselves
neglected or insignificant. Thus they are able to bear the
difficulties of life more easily than others who find in difficulties only further justification for believing themselves
weak and inadequate. In the more difficult situations the
optimists remain quiet in the conviction that mistakes can
always be rectified.

Optimists may immediately be recognized by their manner. They are not afraid, they speak openly and freely,
and are neither too modest nor too inhibited. Were we to
describe them in plastic terms we would show them with
open arms, ready to receive their fellow-men. They make
contacts with others easily and have no difficulty in making friends, because they are not mistrustful. Their speech
is not hindered; their attitude, their carriage, their gait,
is natural and easy. Pure examples of this type are seldom found except in the first years of childhood; there are
however, many degrees of optimism and of ability to make
social contacts with which we can well be satisfied.

Quite a different type are the pessimists. It is with them
that we have the greatest problems of education. These are
the individuals who have acquired an "inferiority complex" as a result of the experiences and impressions of their
childhood, for whom all manner of difficulties have vouchsafed the feeling that life is not easy. They always look for
the dark side of life as a result of their pessimistic personal
philosophy, which has been nourished by false treatment
in their childhood. They are much more conscious of the
difficulties of life than are the optimists, and it is easy for

them to lose their courage. Tortured by a feeling of insecurity, they are constantly seeking for support. Their cry for help is echoed in their external behavior, because they cannot stand alone; if they are children, they persistently call to their mothers, or cry for them as soon as separated. This cry for their mothers can sometimes be heard even in their old age.

The abnormal cautiousness of this type can be seen in their timid, and fearful, external attitude. The pessimists are forever reckoning with the possible dangers which they imagine immediately in the offing. Obviously individuals of this type sleep badly. Sleep, as a matter of fact, is an excellent standard for measuring the development of a human being, for sleep disturbances are an index of greater cautiousness in the face of a feeling of insecurity. It is as though these human beings were ever on guard in order to better defend themselves against the menace of life. How little joy in life, and what poor understanding of it, is to be found in this type! An individual who cannot sleep well has developed but a poor technique of living. Were he really correct in his conclusions, he would not dare to sleep at all. If life were as bitter as he believes it, then sleep actually were a very poor arrangement. In the tendency to approach these natural phenomena of life in a hostile manner the pessimist betrays his unpreparedness for living. Sleep itself need not be disturbed. We may suspect this same pessimistic tendency when we find an individual constantly occupied with investigating whether the doors of his room have been carefully locked, or filling his sleep with dreams of burglars and robbers. Indeed, the type may be recognized by the posture which it assumes in sleeping. Very often individuals who belong to this group curl up into the smallest possible space or sleep with the covers drawn up over their heads.

Human beings may also be divided into assailants and defendants. The assailant attitude is characterized by violent movements. People of the aggressive type, when they

are courageous, elevate courage into foolhardiness, in order
to vehemently attest their capabilities to the world, thus
betraying the deep feeling of insecurity which rules them.
If they are anxious they attempt to harden themselves
against fear. They play the "manly" rôle to a ludicrous
degree. Others go to great pains to suppress all feelings of
tenderness and softness because such feelings appear as
signs of weakness to them. The aggressives show traits of
brutality and cruelty, and, should they tend to pessimism,
all the relationships to environment are changed, for they
have neither the ability to sympathize nor to cooperate, being hostile to the whole world. Their conscious sense of their
own value may at the same time have reached a very high
degree. They may be puffed up with pride and arrogance
and a feeling of their own worth. They exhibit their vani-
ties as though they were actually conquerors, yet the ob-
viousness with which they do all this, and the superfluity
of their movements, not only causes a disharmony in their
relation to the world, but also betrays their whole character,
an artificial superstructure based upon an insecure shifting foundation. Their aggressive attitude, which may last
for a long time, originates in this manner.

Their subsequent development is not easy. Human society does not look with favor upon such beings. The very
fact that they are so much in evidence makes them dis-
liked. In their persistent efforts to win the upper hand, they
soon find themselves in conflict, especially with others of
their own type, whose competition they awaken. Life becomes a chain of battles for them; and when they suffer
the defeats which are unavoidable, their whole line of triumph and victory comes to an abrupt end. They are easily
frightened, cannot sustain their powers for long conflicts,
and are unable to recoup their defeats.

Their failure to accomplish their tasks has a retroactive
influence upon them and their development stops approximately at that place where another type, that type which

feels itself assailed, begins. Individuals of the second type are the assailed, constantly on the defense. They compensate for their feeling of insecurity, not along the line of aggression, but by means of anxiety, precaution, and cowardice. We may be certain that this second attitude never occurs without the previous, and unsuccessful, maintenance of the aggressive attitude which we have just described. The defendant type is quickly appalled by unfortunate experiences. From these they deduce such annihilating consequences that they are easily thrown into flight. Occasionally they succeed in disguising their defection by acting as though a useful piece of work lay along the line of retreat.

Thus when they occupy themselves with remembrances, and develop their fantasy, they actually seek only to avoid the reality which threatens them. Some of them when they have not entirely lost their initiative may actually accomplish something which may not be without general usefulness for society. Many artists belong to this type. They have withdrawn themselves from reality and built themselves a second world in the realm of fantasy and ideals, in which there are no barriers. These artists are the exceptions to the rule. Individuals of this type usually capitulate to difficulties and suffer defeat after defeat. They fear everything and everybody, become increasingly distrustful, and await nothing but hostility on the part of the world.

In our civilization unfortunately their attitude is all too frequently reinforced by the bad experiences at the hands of others; soon they lose all belief in the good qualities of human beings and in the brighter side of life. One of the most common and characteristic traits of such individuals is their external critical attitude. So accentuated does this become at times, that they are quick to recognize the most insignificant defect in others. They set themselves up as judges of humanity without ever doing anything useful themselves for those with whom they live. They busy themselves in criticising and spoiling the other fellow's game. Their mistrust forces them into an anxious, hesitating attitude, yet no sooner are they faced with a task than they begin to doubt and to hesitate, as though they wished to avoid every decision. If we want to portray this type symbolically, we can do so by imagining a man with one hand raised to defend himself and the other covering his eyes, so that he may not see the danger.

Such individuals have other unpleasant character traits. It is well known that those who do not trust themselves never trust others. Envy and avarice are inevitably developed by such an attitude. The isolation in which such doubters live usually signifies their disinclination to prepare pleasures for others, or to join in the happiness of their fellows. Moreover, the happiness of strangers is well-nigh painful to them. Certain members of this group may succeed in maintaining a feeling of their own superiority over the rest of mankind by a trick which is so effective that it is difficult to destroy. In their desire to maintain their superiority at all costs they may develop a behavior pattern so complicated that, at first glance, one would never suspect them of an essential hostility to mankind.

IV. Temperament and Endocrine Secretion

The category of "temperaments" is an old classification of psychic phenomena and traits. It is difficult to know just what is meant by "temperament." Is it the quickness with which one thinks, speaks, or acts? The power or the rhythm with which one approaches a task? On investigation the explanations of psychologists concerning the essence of temperament seem singularly inadequate. We must admit that science has been unable to get away from the concept that there are four temperaments, a concept which dates back to the gray antiquity in which men first began to study the psychic life. The division of temperaments into sanguine, choleric, melancholic, and phlegmatic, dates from ancient Greece, where it was assumed by Hippocrates, whence it was taken up later by the Romans, and remains today an honorable and sacred relic in our present psychology.

To the sanguine type belong those individuals who evince a certain joy in life, who do not take things too seriously, who do not let gray hairs grow too easily on their heads, who attempt to see the pleasantest and most beautiful side of every event, who are sad when sadness is proper, without breaking down, who experience pleasure in happy things, without losing their sense of perspective. A careful description of these individuals shows nothing more than that they are approximately healthy people, in whom high-grade defects are not present. We cannot make this assertion of the other three types.

The choleric individual is described in an old poetical work as a man who fiercely kicks aside a stone which lies in his way, while the sanguine individual comfortably walks around it. Translated into the language of Individual Psychology, the choleric individual is one whose striving for power is so tense that he makes more emphatic and violent movements, feeling that he is forced at all times to produce evidence of his power. He is interested only in overcoming all obstacles in a straight-line aggressive approach. In reality, the more intense movements of these individuals begin early in their childhood, where they lack a feeling of their power, and must demonstrate it constantly to be convinced of its existence.

The melancholic type makes quite a different impression. To maintain the simile which we have mentioned, the melancholic individual, on seeing the stone, would remember all his sins, begin brooding sadly about his past life, and turn back. Individual Psychology sees in him the outspokenly hesitating neurotic who has no confidence in ever overcoming his difficulties or of getting ahead, who prefers not to risk a new adventure, who would rather remain standing still than to proceed to a goal; if such an individual does go on, he begins every movement with the greatest caution. In his life, doubt plays a predominant rôle. This type of man thinks much more of himself than of the others, which eventually excludes him from the greater possibility of finding adequate contacts with life. He is so oppressed with his own cares that he can stare only into the past, or spend his time in fruitless introspection.

The phlegmatic individual in general is a stranger to life. He gathers impressions without deducing the appropriate conclusions from them. Nothing makes a great impression upon him, he is hardly interested in anything, he makes no friends, in short he has almost no connections with life: of all types he perhaps stands at the greatest distance from the business of living.

We may therefore conclude that the sanguine individual alone can be a good human being. Clearly defined temperaments however are seldom found. For the most part one deals with admixtures of one or more, and this very circumstance robs the lore of temperament of all value. Nor are these "types" and "temperaments" fixed. We find, frequently, that one temperament dissolves into another, as when a child who begins as a choleric individual, later becomes melancholic, and ends his life the picture of the phlegmatic habitus. The sanguine individual seems to be that one who has been least exposed to the feeling of inferiority in his childhood, who has shown fewest important bodily infirmities, and has been subjected to no strong irritations, with the result that he developed quietly, with a certain love for life, which enables him to approach it on a sure footing.

At this point science enters the lists and declares: "Temperaments are dependent upon the glands of internal secretion."[1] One of the latest developments in medical science

[1] Cf. Kretschmer's *Character and Temperament*—Berlin 1921.

has been the recognition of the importance of endocrine secretions. The glands of internal secretion are the thyroid, the pituitary, the adrenals, the parathyroids, and the islands of Langerhans in the pancreas, the interstitial glands of the testes and ovaries, together with certain other histological structures, the functions of which are but vaguely understood. These glands have no ducts but pour their secretions directly into the blood.

The general impression is that all organs and tissues are influenced in their growth and activity by these endocrine secretions which are carried by the blood to every single cell in the body. These secretions act as activators or detoxicants and are essential to life, but the full significance of these endocrine glands is still veiled in darkness. The whole science of endocrine secretion is only in its beginnings and positive facts concerning the function of the endocrine juices are few and far between. But since this young science has demanded recognition, and has attempted to direct the line of psychological thought as regards character and temperament, in affirming that these secretions determine character and temperament, we must say something more about them.

To begin with, let us deal with one important objection. If we see an actual disease process, such as cretinism, in which the thyroid gland is deficiently active, it is quite true that we also find psychic manifestations, comparable to the last degree of the phlegmatic temperament. Without going into the fact that these individuals appear puffy and bloated, that the growth of their hair is pathological, and that they develop a particularly thick skin, they show extraordinary slowness and lassitude in their movements. Their psychic sensitivity is markedly lessened and their initiative is almost absent.

Should we now compare this case with another case which we could designate as phlegmatic, although no demonstrable pathological changes in the thyroid gland were present, we should find two entirely different pictures, with entirely dissimilar character traits. One might therefore say that seemingly there is something in the secretion of the thyroid gland which helps to maintain an adequate psychic function; we cannot, however, go so far as to say that the phlegmatic temperament *arises* out of the loss of this secretion of the thyroid gland.

The pathologically phlegmatic type is something entirely different from that which we are used to calling phlegmatic; the *psychologically* phlegmatic character and temperament is distinguished from the *pathologically* phlegmatic, entirely by the previous psychological history of the individual. The phlegmatic types with which we as psychologists are interested are by no means static individuals. We shall often be surprised to find what astonishingly deep and violent reactions sometimes occur in them. There is no phlegmatic individual who has been phlegmatic all his life. We will learn that his temperament is but an artificial shell, a defense mechanism (for which he may have had, conceivably, a constitutionally determined tendency in his life) which an oversensitive being has created for himself, a fortification which he has thrown up between himself and the outer world. The phlegmatic temperament is a defense mechanism, a meaningful response to the challenge of existence, and in this sense entirely dissimilar to the senseless slowness, indolence, and inadequacy of a cretin whose thyroid gland is completely inadequate.

Even in those cases in which it would seem that only those patients who previously had an incompetent thyroid secretion acquired a phlegmatic temperament, this important and significant objection is not over-ruled. This is not the crux of the whole question. What actually is at stake is a whole complex bundle of causes and purposes, a whole system of organ activity plus external influences, which produce a feeling of inferiority. From this feeling of inferiority originates the attempt of the individual who *can* develop a phlegmatic temperament, to shield himself from unpleasant insults and injuries to his personal self esteem, in this way. But this means only that we are here dealing specifically with a type of whom we have already spoken in general. Here the deficiency of the thyroid gland is a specific organ inferiority, and its consequences assume a dominant rôle. And this organ inferiority gives rise to a more strained attitude toward life for which the individual attempts compensation through psychic tricks, of which the phlegmatic habitus is a well known example.

We shall be confirmed in our conception when we take into consideration other anomalies of internal secretion and examine the temperaments which belong to them. Thus there are individuals who have an exaggerated thyroid secretion, as in Basedow's disease, or goiter. The physical signs of this disease are over-activity of the heart, high pulse-frequency, exophthalmos or bulging eyes, swelling of the thyroid gland, and the greater or lesser tendency of the extremities, particularly the hands, to tremble. Such patients perspire easily, and their gastro-intestinal apparatus frequently labors under greater difficulties as a result of the secondary influence of the thyroid secretion upon that of the pancreas. Such patients are highly sensitive and easily irritated, and they are marked by a hasty, irritated, trembling activity, often associated with well marked anxiety states. The picture of a typical exophthalmic goiter patient is unmistakably that of an over-anxious human being.

To say, however, that this is identical with the picture of psychological anxiety, is to commit a grave error. The psychological phenomena which one sees in exophthalmic goiter, the anxiety states, the inability to do certain bodily or mental work, the easy fatigue and great weakness, are conditioned not only by psychic causes, but also by organic ones. A comparison with a human being who suffers from a hurry and anxiety neurosis shows an immense contrast. In marked contrast to those individuals whose psychic over-activity is a result of hyperthyroidism, whose character is secondary to a chronic intoxication, who are so to speak drunk on thyroid secretion are those other excitable, hasty, anxious individuals who belong in an entirely different category, for their position is determined almost entirely by their previous psychic experiences. The hyperthyroid individual certainly shows *similarities* in behavior, but his activity lacks that *planfulness* and *purposefulness* which is the essential index of character and temperament.

Other glands with internal secretion must also be discussed here. The connection between the development of the various glands of internal secretion and the development of the testes and ovaries is especially important.[1] Our contention which has become one of the fundamental tenets of biological research, is that one never finds anomalies of the glands of internal secretion without also finding anomalies of the gonads, or sexual glands. The especial dependency, and the reason for the simultaneous appearance of these inferiorities, has never been fully determined. In the case of organic defects in these glands too, the same conclusions which we might have been led to deduce in other organic inferiorities, are to be drawn. Where the gonads are insufficient we find an individual with organic difficulties who finds it more difficult to adjust himself to life, and in consequence must produce a greater number of psychic tricks and defense mechanisms to aid him in making the adjustment.

Enthusiastic investigators of the endocrine glands have led us to expect that character and temperament were wholly dependent upon the endocrine secretions of the sexual glands. It appears however, that extensive anomalies in the glandular substance of the testes and ovaries are infrequently found. In those cases where pathological de-

[1] Cf. Alfred Adler, *Organ Inferiority and Its Psychic Compensation*—Adler, *Studie uber die Minderwertigkeit von Organen.*

generations are present, we are dealing with the exceptional cases. There is no particular psychic habitus which is directly connected with the defective *function* of the sexual glands, which would not originate much more frequently in the specific diseases of the sexual glands; we find no solid medical foundation for an endocrine basis of character such as the endocrinologists claim. That certain stimuli, necessary for the vitality of the organism, arise from the sexual glands, and that these stimuli may determine the position of the child in his environment, is undeniable. Yet these stimuli may be produced by other organs as well, and they are not necessarily the basis of a specific psychic structure.

Since putting a value on a human being is a difficult and delicate task, in which an error may decide between life and death, we must issue a warning here. The temptation on the part of children who come into the world with congenitally weak organs to acquire particular psychic tricks and artifices as a compensation is very great. *But this temptation to develop a peculiar psychic structure can be overcome.* There is no organ, no matter in what condition it is, which would necessarily and irrevocably force an individual to some particular attitude in life. It may dishearten him, but that is another matter. View points similar to that we have just mentioned can exist solely because no one has ever attempted to obviate the difficulties in the psychic development of children with organic inferiorities. One has allowed them to lapse into errors as a result of their inferiorities; one has examined and observed them, but not attempted to help, or to stimulate them! The new *positional* or *contexual* psychology which has been founded upon the experiences of Individual Psychology will prove its rightness in consequence of its teachings on this score, and will force the present *dispositional* or *constitutional* psychology to strike its colors.

CHAPTER II

AGGRESSIVE CHARACTER TRAITS

I. Vanity and Ambition

As soon as the striving for recognition assumes the upper hand, it evokes a condition of greater tension in the psychic life. As a consequence, the goal of power and superiority becomes increasingly obvious to the individual, who pursues it with movements of great intensity and violence, and his life becomes the expectation of a great triumph. Such an individual loses his sense of reality because he loses his connection with life, being always occupied with the question of what other people think about him, and being concerned chiefly with the impression that he makes. The freedom of his action is inhibited to an extraordinary degree through this style of life, and his most obvious character trait becomes vanity.

It is probable that every human being is vain to some degree; yet making an exhibit of one's vanity is not considered good form. Vanity, therefore, is frequently so disguised and cloaked that it appears in the most varied transformations. There is a type of modesty, by way of example, which is essentially vain. One man may be so vain as never to consider the judgment of others; another seeks greedily after public approbation and uses it to his own advantage.

Exaggerated beyond a certain degree vanity becomes exceedingly dangerous. Quite beside the fact that vanity leads an individual to all kinds of useless work and effort which is more concerned with the *semblance* of things than with their *essence,* and beside the fact that it causes him to think constantly of himself, or at the most only of other people's opinion of him, its greatest danger is that it leads him sooner or later to lose contact with reality. He loses his understanding for human connections, his relations to life become warped. He forgets the obligations of living, and he loses sight especially of the contributions which nature demands of every man. No other vice is so well designed to stunt the free development of a human being as that personal vanity which forces an individual to approach every event and every fellow with the query: "What do I get out of this?"

People are wont to help themselves out of the difficulty by substituting the better-sounding word "ambition" for vanity, or haughtiness. How many people there are who are exceedingly proud to tell us how ambitious they are! The concept "energetic" or "active" is also frequently used. So long as this energy proves itself of use for society we can admit its value, but it is usually the rule that all these terms "industry," "activity," "energy," and "go-getting" are expressions to cloak an unusual degree of vanity.

Vanity very soon prevents an individual from playing the game according to the rules. Much more frequently it causes him to be a disturber of others so that those individuals who are excluded from the satisfaction of their own vanity are often to be found striving to prevent others from the full expression of their lives. Children whose vanity is in process of growth exhibit their valor in dangerous situations and like to show weaker children how powerful they are. A case in point is cruelty to animals. Other children who are already discouraged to a certain degree will attempt to satisfy their vanity with all manner of incomprehensible pettinesses. They will avoid the main arena of work and attempt to satisfy their striving for significance by playing an heroic rôle in some side show of life which their mood may have dictated. The people who are always complaining how bitter life is, and how badly

fate has treated them, belong in this category. They are
the ones who would let us know that if they had not been
so badly educated, or if some other misfortune had not
occurred to them, that they would be the leaders of today.
They are constantly making alibis for not approaching the
real firing front of life; the sole satisfaction for their vanity may be found in the dreams which they create for themselves.

The objection has frequently been made that without
great ambition the great accomplishments of mankind
would never have taken place. This is a false view in a
false perspective. Since no one is entirely free of vanity,
everyone has a certain amount of it. But it is not this
vanity, surely, which is responsible for determining the
direction his activity has taken toward universal usefulness,
nor has it given him the power to carry out his great accomplishments! Such *accomplishments can occur only under the stimulus of a social feeling*. A work of genius
becomes valuable only through its social connotation.
Whatever vanity is present in its creation can only detract
from its value, and disturb its creation; in a real work of
genius the influence of vanity is not great.

There are people who are deeply convinced that they
are not vain. They look only at the outside, knowing that
vanity lies much deeper. Vanity may be expressed, for instance, in that a person always demands the full stage in
his social circle, must always have the floor, or judges a
social gathering as good or bad according to his ability to
maintain the center of the stage. Other individuals of this
same sort never go into society, and seek to avoid it as
much as possible. This avoidance of society may express
itself in various ways. Non-acceptance of invitations, or
coming late, or forcing one's host to coax and flatter before
one comes, are some of these vain tricks. Other individuals
go into society only under very definite conditions and
show their vanity by being very "exclusive." They proudly

consider this as a laudable trait. Others, again show their vanity by wishing to be present at *all* social gatherings.

One must not feel that these are unimportant and insignificant details; they are very deeply rooted in the soul. In reality a person who can be guilty of them has not much place in his personality for the social feeling; he is more apt to be a destroyer of society, than its friend. The poetical powers of a great writer were necessary in order to portray these types with all their variations. We attempt solely to indicate them in their bare outlines.

The one motive which we can discover in all vanity indicates that the vain individual has created a goal which is impossible of attainment in this life. It is his purpose to be more than all others in the world, and this goal is the result of his feeling of inadequacy. We may suspect that anyone whose vanity is well marked, has little sense of his own worth. There may be individuals who are conscious that their vanity begins where their feeling of inadequacy becomes evident, but unless they make a fruitful use of their knowledge their mere consciousness is sterile.

Vanity develops at a very early period. There is usually something very puerile about all vanity, and as a result, vain individuals always impress us as being somewhat childish. The situations which may determine the development of vanity are varied. In one case a child feels himself neglected because, as a result of inadequate education, he senses his littleness as unbearably oppressive. Other children acquire a certain haughtiness as a result of their family tradition. We can be certain their parents, too, assumed such an "aristocratic" bearing, which distinguished them from others, and made them very proud.

Occasionally, capable, important individuals who have developed themselves to the highest degree are to be found in this type. If they were to throw their talents into the scales, they might be of some value, but they misuse their abilities in order to intoxicate themselves further. The conditions which they set for an active cooperation with society are not easily satisfied. They may, for instance, place unfulfillable conditions on time, pointing to the fact that they *used* to do things, or *had* learned things, or *had* known other things; again, they make alibis, saying that others *had* done or had *not* done things, according to their system. Their conditions may be impossible of satisfaction because of still more evanescent reasons. They will assert, for instance, that all would have gone well if men were really men, or if women had not been what they were. But these conditions could not be fulfilled even with the best intentions! We must conclude, therefore, that they are really only lazy alibis as valuable as hypnotic or intoxicant drugs which rob one of the necessity of having to think about the time one has wasted.

There is a great deal of hostility in these people, and they are inclined to take the pain and sorrow of others lightly. This is the mechanism whereby they achieve a feeling of greatness. La Rochefoucault, a great knower of human nature, said of most people "They can bear the pains of others easily." Social hostility often expresses itself in the assumption of a sharp, critical manner. These enemies of society are forever blaming, criticizing, ridiculing, judging, and condemning the world. They are dissatisfied with everything. But it is not enough only to recognize the bad, and condemn it! One must ask oneself: "What have I done to make these things better?"

The derogatory, deprecating fashion of such individuals, who cannot criticize too much, is their expression of a character trait which is common enough. We have called this the deprecation complex. It indicates actually what the point of attack of the vain person is: it is the worth and value of his fellow man. The deprecation tendency is an attempt to create the feeling of superiority by the degradation of one's fellows. The recognition of another's worth is equivalent to an insult to the vain one's personality.

From this fact alone we can draw far reaching conclusions, and learn how deeply rooted in the personality of a vain individual his feeling of weakness and inadequacy is.

Since no one of us is quite free of this taint we can use this discussion very well to apply a standard to ourselves, even though we are not capable of uprooting, in a short time, what thousands of years of tradition has allowed to grow up in us. It will nevertheless be a step in advance if we will not allow ourselves to be hoodwinked and entangled in prejudices which eventually will be proven disadvantageous and dangerous. It is not our desire to be different human beings, nor to seek different human beings. Yet we feel that a natural law demands that we stretch out our hands to join, and cooperate with, our fellow-men. In an age like ours which demands so much cooperation, there is no longer place for the strivings of personal vanity. It is in just such an epoch as ours that the contradictions of a vain attitude toward life appear especially obvious and crass, since we see daily how vanity leads to failure, and eventually brings its bearers under the severe fire of society, or places them in need of that society's sympathy. At no time was vanity more objectionable than today. The least we can do is search for better forms and manifestations of vanity, so that if we must be vain, we will at least exercise our vanity in the direction of the common weal!

The following case is an excellent demonstration of the dynamics of vanity. A young woman, the youngest of several sisters, was very much pampered from the earliest days of her life. Her mother was at her service day and night, and satisfied her every wish. As a result of this solicitude the demands of this youngest child, who was very weak physically, as well, mounted into the realm of the immeasurable. One fine day she made the discovery that her mother lorded it over her environment whenever she was sick; and it did not take the young lady long to learn that sickness might be a very valuable asset.

She soon swallowed the disinclination which normal healthy people feel toward sickness, and it was not at all unpleasant for her to feel badly, from time to time. Soon she acquired so much training in being sick that she could easily be ill whenever she desired it, and especially when her heart was set upon attaining some special object. Unfortunately she was constantly desirous of obtaining some special object, with the result that, so far as her environment was concerned, she became chronically ill. The manifestations of this "sickness complex" in children and grown-ups who feel their power growing, and are enabled to occupy the center of their families, and exercise an unbounded domination over them by virtue of their illness, are many. When we have to deal with tender, weak individuals the possibilities of this way to power are enormous, and naturally it is just such individuals who find this way to power, since they have already tasted the concern which their relatives show for their health.

In such a situation an individual can play certain accessory tricks to gain his ends. By way of beginning, for instance, one does not eat enough; the result is one looks badly, and the family must go to great lengths to cook delicacies for its sick member, and presto!, in the process, the desire to have someone constantly dancing attendance upon one develops. These are the people who cannot bear to be alone. Simply by feeling ill, or being in danger, one acquires the beloved attention. This is easily arranged by identifying oneself with a dangerous situation, or with some sickness.

The ability to identify oneself with a thing or situation we call empathy. It is well demonstrated in our dreams in which we feel *as though* some specific situation actually was taking place. Once the victims of the "sickness complex" assume that mode of acquiring power, they succeed very easily in producing and conjuring up a feeling of malaise so cleverly that there can be no talk of a lie, or distortion, or imagination. We know very well that the identification with a situation can produce the same effect as if that situation were actually present. We know that such individuals can actually vomit, or produce a real feeling of anxiety, just as though they actually were nauseated or in danger. Usually they betray themselves in the manner in which they produce these symptoms; this young woman of whom we were speaking, for instance, declared that she sometimes had a fear "as if I would have an apoplectic stroke any moment." There are people who can imagine a thing so clearly that they actually lose their equilibrium, and one cannot talk of imagination or simulation. All that is necessary is that one of these sickness champions succeeds once in impressing his environment with the signs of a disease, or at least with so-called "nervous" symptoms. Thereafter everyone who has once been impressed must remain at the side of the "patient," take care of him, and attend to his well being. The sickness of a fellow man challenges the social feeling of every normal human being. This fact is misused and constituted into a basis of a feeling of power by individuals of the type which we have just described.

The opposition to the laws of society and communal life which demand such far reaching considerations of one's fellow men, becomes very evident under such circumstances. We shall find as a rule that these individuals whom we have been describing are unable to understand the pain or happiness of their fellow-men. It will be difficult for them not to injure the rights of their neighbors; to be helpful to their fellows is entirely beyond their interests. Occasionally they may succeed in life, as a result of terrific efforts, and by virtue of the mobilization of their entire armament of education and culture; more often their efforts will be directed towards attaining only the outward show of interest in the welfare of their fellows. Essentially, nothing but self love and vanity is the basis of their conduct.

Certainly this is true of the young woman we have just described. Her solicitude for her relative seemingly exceeded all bounds. If her mother were to bring her breakfast to her bed, half an hour late, it would cause her to be worried and concerned; under such circumstances she was not satisfied until she had awakened her husband, and forced him to investigate whether something had not happened to her mother. In the course of time her mother accustomed herself to appear very punctually with the young woman's breakfast. Much the same thing happened to her husband. Being a business man, he had to consider his customers and business associates to some extent, yet every time he appeared at home a few minutes late he found his wife almost on the verge of a nervous breakdown, shivering with anxiety, bathed in perspiration, bitterly complaining how she had been the prey of the most horrible apprehensions and presentiments. Her poor husband could but follow the example of her mother and force himself to be punctual.

Many people will object that this woman really got no benefit from her actions and that these in reality were no great triumphs. One must keep in mind that we have described but a small part of the whole; her sickness is a danger sign which says, "Take care!" It is an index of all the other relationships in her life. With this simple device she put everyone in her environment into training. The satisfaction of her vanity played an essential rôle in the satisfaction of her boundless desire to dominate her environment. Imagine the length to which such an individual must go to accomplish his purpose! We must deduce that her attitude and behavior had become an utter *necessity* for her when we realize what a high price she was paying for them! She could not live quietly unless her words were obeyed unconditionally and punctually. But marriage consists in more than having one's husband punctual. A thousand other relationships are fixed by the imperative conduct of this woman, who has learned how to reinforce her commands with anxiety states. She is seemingly intensely concerned with the welfare of others, yet everyone must unconditionally obey her will. We can make only one conclusion, her solicitude is an instrument for the satisfaction of her vanity.

It is not unusual to find a psychic attitude of this nature assuming such proportions that the accomplishment of a person's will becomes more important than the thing which he desires. This is exemplified by the case of a six-year-old girl whose egotism was so boundless that she was concerned solely with the accomplishment of any random whim that happened to be in her thought at any particular moment. Her behavior was permeated by the desire to show her powers in the conquest of her associates. This conquest usually was the result of her activity. Her mother, who was very anxious to remain on good terms with her daughter, once attempted to surprise the child with her favorite dessert, bringing it to her with the words, "I have brought you this dessert because I know that you like it so much." The little girl crashed the plate to the ground, trampled on the cake and cried out, "But I don't want it because *you* are giving it to me, I want it only when *I* want it." Another time this same mother asked whether this little girl would like to have coffee or milk for lunch. The little girl stood in the doorway and murmured very clearly, "If she says coffee I will drink milk, and if she says milk I will drink coffee!"

This was a child who spoke her mind plainly, but there are many children who are in the same class who do not express their thoughts so distinctly. Perhaps every child has this trait to a degree and is at great odds to accomplish its will, even though it has nothing to gain, and may even suffer pain and unhappiness as a result of having its own way. For the most part these will be the children in whom the privilege of having their own way has been allowed to develop. Opportunities for this are not hard to find nowadays. Consequently among adults we will find people who are anxious to have their own way much more frequently than those who desire to help their fellows. Some go so far in their vanity that they are incapable of doing anything which another has suggested to them, even though this is the most self-understood procedure in the world, and really signifies their own happiness. These are the people who cannot wait until another has finished speaking in order to raise their objections and their opposition. And there are some people whose will is spurred on by their vanity to such an extent that they actually say "no!" when they want to say "yes!"

To have one's own way all the time is possible only within the circle of one's family, and not always there. Individuals whose contacts with strangers are amiable and complaisant are often to be found. This contact does not last long, however, is quickly broken off, and surely sought for but seldom. Since life is as it is, and human beings are constantly being brought together, it is not unusual to find some such individual who wins the hearts of all, but once having won them, leaves them in the lurch. Many strive constantly to circumscribe their activities within the circle of their family life. This process occurred in the case of our patient. As a consequence of her charming character she was known outside of her home as a delightful person, was universally beloved, but whenever she left her home, she returned very soon. The desire to return to her family was indicated by a variety of tricks. If she went to a party she got a headache (because at any social gathering she could not maintain the feeling of her absolute power to the degree which she was capable of maintaining at home), and had to return. Since this woman could not solve the main problem of her life, the problem of the satisfaction of her vanity, except in the center of her family life, she was forced to arrange something to drive her back to this family whenever necessary. She carried on to the extent that she was seized by anxiety and excitement every time that she went among strangers. Soon she could not go to the theater, and, finally, she could not appear upon the street because in these situations she lost the feeling that the whole world was subject to her will. The situation which she sought was not to be found outside of her family and particularly not upon the street; as a result she declared her disinclination to appear outside of her home except when accompanied by the persons of her "court." This was the ideal situation which she loved: to be surrounded constantly by solicitous people who were occupied with her welfare. As the examination showed she had carried this pattern with her from early childhood.

She was the youngest, the weakest, the sickest, and was under the necessity of being more pampered and cared for than the others. She seized upon the situation of the pampered child, and would have maintained it at all costs throughout her life had she not disturbed the inexorable conditions of life which are sharply opposed to this type of behavior. Her unrest and her anxiety states, which were so outspoken that no one could deny them, betrayed the fact that she had become side-tracked in the solution of her vanity problem. The solution was inadequate because she did not have the will to subordinate herself to the conditions of social life and thus, finally, the manifestations of her inability to solve this problem became so painful that she sought the help of a physician.

Now it was necessary to unveil the whole super-structure of her life which she had so carefully constructed during the course of many years. Great resistances had to be overcome because essentially she was not prepared to change, though outwardly she appealed to the physician for help. What she really desired was to keep on ruling her family as before, without having to pay the price of the torturing anxiety states which pursued her upon the streets. But one was not to be had without the other! She was shown how she was a prisoner within the cage of her own unconscious behavior whose advantages she wished to enjoy, but whose disadvantages she wished to avoid.

This example shows all too clearly how every considerable degree of vanity acts as a continuous load throughout life, inhibits the full development of a human being, and finally leads to his breakdown. The patient cannot understand these things clearly so long as his attention is directed only to its advantages. For this reason so many people are convinced that their ambition, which might more appropriately be called vanity, is a valuable characteristic because they do not understand that this character trait constantly dissatisfies a human being, and robs him of his rest and sleep.

It is quite a different thing when the reputation of a man is justified by his services to others. His honor then comes to him of itself, and if it is opposed by others, their opposition has little weight. He can remain quietly in the possession of his honor because he has not staked everything upon vanity. The deciding point is the egoistic attitude, the constant search for the elevation of one's own personality. The vain rôle is always that of expectation and acquisition. Contrast your vain person with that other individual who shows a well developed social feeling, who goes through life with the question, "What can I give?", and you will see the enormous differences in character and in value immediately.

And so we arrive at the point of view which people have understood for thousands of years. It is expressed in a famous Biblical line: "It is more blessed to give than to receive." If we reflect over the meaning of these words, the expression of great experience in human nature, we recognize that it is the attitude and mood of giving which is meant here. It is the mood of giving, or serving, of helping, which brings with itself a certain compensation and psychic harmony, like the gift of the gods which takes root in him who gives it away!

On the other hand the acquisitive people are usually discontented, being occupied solely with the thought of what they must still achieve and still possess, in order to be happy. The acquisitive man, whose look is never directed toward the necessities and needs of others, and to whom the misfortune of others is a joy, has no place in his system for reconciliation and peace with life. He demands the unbending submission of others to laws which his egoism has dictated. He demands a different heaven from the one which exists, a different way of thinking and feeling; in short, his dissatisfaction and immodesty are as execrable as everything else which is characteristic of him.

There are the other and more primitive forms of vanity which we find in those people who dress conspicuously, or with a certain sense of their own importance, who deck themselves out like monkeys in order to make a brave appearance, in much the same way that primitive man attempts to shine by wearing an especially long feather in his hair when he has reached a certain degree of pride and honor. There are a number of human beings who find the greatest satisfaction in always being dressed beautifully, and according to the latest fashion. The various ornaments which such individuals carry indicate their vanity just as much as so many standards, belligerent emblems, or weapons, whose purpose, when rightly understood, is to scare off the enemy. Sometimes this vanity is expressed by erotic emblems, or by tatooing which seems frivolous to us. In these cases we have a feeling that the individual is striving to make an impression, though he can do so only at the cost of shamelessness. Shameless behavior lends the feeling of greatness and superiority to some; others again have this same feeling when they appear hard, brutal, stubborn, or isolated. In reality these may be individuals who are closer to tenderness than to bad manners, whose quondam brutality is but a pose. In boys especially we find a seeming lack of feeling which is, in effect, a hostile attitude toward the social feeling. Individuals who are impelled by this type of vanity, who desire to play a rôle through which others suffer, would be insulted by any appeal to their finer feelings. Such an appeal would simply cause them to stiffen their attitude. We have seen cases in which the parents approach a child, pleading their pain, while the child whom they approach actually acquires a feeling of his own superiority from the demonstrations of their sorrows.

We have already noted that vanity likes to mask itself. Vain people who would like to rule others must first catch them in order to bind them to themselves. We must not, therefore, allow ourselves to be entirely duped by the amiability, or friendliness, and willingness to make contacts, which a person may show; nor must we be deceived into believing that he may not nevertheless be a belligerent aggressor who is looking for conquests, and to the maintenance of his personal superiority. The first phase of this battle must be to assure one's opponent and cajole him so far that he loses his caution. In the first phase, that of friendly approach, one is easily tempted to believe that the aggressor is an individual with a great deal of social feeling; the second serves to remove the veils and show us our error. These are the people who disappoint us. We believe that they possess two souls, but it is but the one soul, which makes an amiable approach but effects a bitter ending.

The technique of approach may go so far as to assume the proportions of a sport: soul catching. The traits of the uttermost devotion may be evident, constituting in themselves, a certain kind of triumph. These people speak glibly of humanity, and seemingly show love of their fellows in their actions. Yet this usually occurs in so demonstrative a fashion, that the real knower of the human soul becomes wary. An Italian criminal psychologist has said, "when the ideal attitude of a human being goes beyond a certain degree, when his philanthropy and humanity assume conspicuous proportions, we may well be distrustful." Naturally we must take this phrase with reservations, but we may be quite sure that the point of view is valid. In general we can easily recognise the type. Bootlicking is not pleasant to any one. It soon becomes uncomfortable, and one is on one's guard against people who make use of this form of flattery. We should rather be inclined to contra-indicate this method to ambitious people. It is better to choose a different approach and a smoother technique!

We have already become acquainted in the first part of our book with those situations which most frequently cause deviations from the normal psychic development. From an educational standpoint the difficulties lie in the fact that we are dealing, in such cases, with children who have assumed a belligerent attitude toward their environment. Even though the teacher knows his duties, which are deeply based in the logic of life, he cannot make this logic obligatory to the child. The only possible way of doing this would seem to lie in avoiding any belligerent situation, so far as possible, and treating the child not as the *object* of education, but as the *subject;* as though he were a fully adult individual who stood on the same footing as the teacher. In this way it would not be so easy for a child to fall into the error of believing that he was under pressure, or was being neglected, and thus under the necessity of taking up the gage of battle with his teachers. From this battle position the false ambition of our culture which characterizes our thinking, our actions, and our character traits to such a large degree, develops automatically and gives occasion, first for increasingly entangled relationships, to defeats of the personality, and finally to the complete disruption and breakdown of the individual.

It is very characteristic that fairy tales, that source from which all of us have learned much of our understanding of human nature, give us a number of examples which show us the danger of vanity. We must here review one fairy tale which shows in a particularly drastic way how the unbridled development of vanity leads to an automatic destruction of the personality. It is Hans Christian Andersen's story of *The Vinegar Jar.* The story goes that a fisherman grants a fish he has caught, its freedom, and the fish, out of gratitude, permits him the fulfillment of a single wish. His wish is fulfilled. The dissatisfied, ambitious wife of the fisherman, however, demands that the fisherman change his humble request and make her first a duchess, then a queen, and finally, God! She sends her fisherman husband back to the fish again and again, until the fish, finally infuriated at the last request, deserts the fisherman forever.

There are no limits to the development of vanity and ambition. It is very interesting to see how in fairy tales, as well as in the overheated psychic striving of vain individuals, the striving for power assumes the expression of a desire for the ideal of God-likeness. One does not have to search far to find that a vain person acts exactly as though he were God (which happens in the most serious cases), or he behaves himself as though he were God's lieutenant, or again, he expresses wishes and desires which only God could fulfill. This manifestation, the striving for God-likeness, is the extreme point of a tendency which is present in all his activities, and amounts to a desire to project himself beyond the boundaries of his personality.

The evidences of this tendency are many in our age. That large group of people that interests itself in spiritualism, psychic research, telepathy and similar movements, is composed of just such people who are anxious to grow beyond the boundaries of mere humanity, who are desirous of possessing powers which human beings do not possess, who

wish to remove themselves beyond time and space, as in
the intercourse with ghosts and the spirits of the dead.

If we investigate still further we shall find that a large
portion of humanity has the tendency to secure for itself
a little place in the vicinity of God. There are still a number of schools whose educational ideal is God-likeness. In
former times this was, indeed, the conscious ideal of all
religious education. We can only attest to the results of this
education with horror. We must certainly look about nowadays for a more reasonable ideal. But that this tendency
is so deeply rooted in human kind is quite conceivable.
Apart from the psychological reasons the fact is that a
large portion of humanity gets its first conception of the
nature of man from the catch-word phrases of the Bible
which declares that man was created in the image of God.
We can imagine what important and what perilous consequences such a conception may leave behind it in the soul
of a child. The Bible, to be sure, is a wonderful work which
one can constantly read and reread with astonishment at
its perspicacity, after one's judgment has matured. But
let us not teach it to children, at least not without a com-
mentary, to the end that a child may learn to be content in
this life, without assuming all manner of magical powers,
and demanding that everyone be his slave, ostensibly because he was created in the image of God!

Closely related to this thirst for God-likeness is the
ideal of the fairy-tale Utopia where every dream comes
true. Children seldom count upon the reality of such fairy
pictures. Yet if we take cognizance of the exceedingly
great interest of children in magic, then we can never
doubt how easily they are allured thereby, and how easy
it is for them to sink themselves in such fantasies. The
idea of enchantment, of a magic influence upon others,
is found to a strong degree in some people, and may not
be lost until they are very old.

On one point perhaps no man is entirely free in his

thoughts: in the matter of the superstitious feeling that women have a magical influence over men. One can find many men who act as though they thought they were exposed to the magical influence of their sexual partners. This superstition leads us back to a time in which this belief was held much more firmly than today. These were the days in which a woman, on the merest pretext, ran the danger of being called a witch or a magician, a prejudice which burdened the whole of Europe like a nightmare, and determined its history in part, for many decades. If one recalls that a million women were the victims of this delusion, one cannot speak any longer simply of harmless mistakes, but must compare the influence of this superstition to the horrors of the Inquisition, or of a world war.

The satisfaction of one's vanity through the misuse of one's desire for religious satisfaction, is also found on the trail of the striving for God-likeness. We have only to remark how important it may be to an individual who has suffered psychic shipwreck, to remove himself from other human beings, and engage in personal conversation with God! Such an individual considers himself quite in the proximity of God, Who is duty-bound, by virtue of the worshipper's pious prayers and orthodox ritual, to personally concern Himself with the worshipper's well-being. Such religious hocus-pocus is usually so far from true religion that it impresses us as being purely psychopathological. We have heard a man say that he could not fall asleep unless he had said some definite prayer, because if he had not sent this prayer to heaven, some human being somewhere would have a misfortune. To understand this whole flimsy soap-bubble-blowing it is but necessary to produce the negative corollary of some such statement, and interpret it. "If I say my prayer no harm can come to him," would be the proposition in this instance. These are the ways in which one can easily achieve a magical greatness. Through this paltry trick a human being really succeeds in diverting a misfortune in the life of another human being at a definite time. In the day-dreams of such religious individuals we can find similar movements which reach out beyond the measure of humanity. In these day-dreams are disclosed empty gestures, brave deeds, which are quite incapable of actually changing the nature of things, but succeed very well in the imagination of the day-dreamer in preventing him from coming into contact with reality.

In our civilization there is one thing which seems to have a magic power, and that is money. Many people believe that you can do anything with money that you may wish. It is not strange therefore that their ambition and vanity occupies itself with the question of money and property alone. Their ceaseless striving for the acquisition of worldly goods now becomes comprehensible. To us it seems almost pathological. Again, nothing but a form of vanity which attempts, by the heaping up of possessions, to produce a certain semblance of the enchanter's power. One of those very wealthy men who, although he should have had quite enough, continued to chase after money, admitted after the beginning of a delusional insanity: "Yes, do you know that (money) is the power which constantly allures me again and again!" This man understood it, but many dare not understand it. The possession of power is so closely allied with the possession of money and property today, and the striving for money and property seems so natural in our civilization, that no one pays any attention to the fact that many of the individuals who do nothing but chase after gold are spurred on by their vanity.

In conclusion we will report another case which will show all the single aspects we have previously discussed, and at the same time give us an understanding of another phenomenon in which vanity plays a great rôle, and that is the condition of delinquency. The case concerns a brother and sister. The brother, who was the younger, was considered untalented, whereas the older sister had a reputation for exceptional ability. When the brother could not maintain the competition any longer he gave up the race. He was pushed into the background although everyone attempted to remove difficulties from his path. At the same time he carried a heavy burden with him which amounted to the seeming acknowledgment that he was untalented. One had taught him from his earliest childhood days that his sister would always conquer the difficulties of life easily, whereas he was fit only for insignificant things. In this way, because of the better position of his sister, people credited him with an inadequacy which actually did not exist.

Burdened with this great load he came to school. His was the career of a pessimistically inclined child who sought to avoid the discovery and recognition of his inability at all costs. As he grew older there arose also the desire not to be forced to play the rôle of the stupid boy, but to be treated like an adult. At the age of fourteen he had often taken part in the society of grown-ups, but his deep feeling of inferiority was a thorn in his side which forced him to consider how he could play the rôle of gentleman who had already grown up.

His path thus led one day into the domain of prostitution, and there he has remained to this time. As the expenditure of money was closely related to his interest in prostitutes, while at the same time his desire to play the grown-up prevented him from begging money of his father, he began to rob his father of any funds he considered necessary. He was not at all pained by these thefts, and he considered himself somewhat in the manner of a grown-up who was the treasurer of his father's money. This continued until one day he was threatened with a severe failure in school. To be demoted would have been an evidence of his inability which he dared not publish.

The following events now occurred: He was suddenly

struck with pangs of remorse and conscience, which interfered sadly with his studies. His situation was bettered by this trick because now, should he fail, he would have an excuse for the world. He was so martyred by his remorse that everyone else in a similar position would also have failed in their studies. At the same time a high degree of distraction hindered him in his studies because it forced him to think of other things. A day was passed in this way, night came and he went to sleep conscious of the fact that he had tried to study, although in reality he was one of those who did not pay the least attention to his work. What happened after this also helped him to carry out his rôle.

He was forced to rise at an early hour. As a result he was sleepy and tired the whole day long and could not pay any attention whatsoever to his work. One certainly could not demand that he compete with his sister! Now it was not his lack of talent which was at fault, but the fatal concomitant phenomena, his remorse, the pangs of conscience, which left him no peace. At last he was armed on all sides and nothing could happen to him. If he failed, there were extenuating circumstances, and no one could say that he was untalented. Should he succeed it was the proof of his ability which no one would admit.

When we see such tricks as these we may be sure that vanity is the cause of them. In this case we can see how far one can expose himself even to the danger of delinquency in order to avoid the discovery of an alleged, but not actually existing, lack of talent. Ambition and vanity produce such complications and side tracks in life. They rob one of all candor and of all true pleasures, of all true joy and happiness in life. Examine more sharply and we find for cause nothing but a stupid mistake!

II. Jealousy

Jealousy is a character trait which is interesting because of its extraordinary frequency. By jealousy is meant not only the jealousy of love relationships, but also the jealousy which is to be found in all other human relationships. Thus, in childhood, we find children who develop jealousy in an attempt to be superior to one another; these same children may also develop ambition, and indicate their belligerent attitude to the world with both these traits. Jealousy, sister of ambition, a character trait which may last a life time, arises from the feeling of being neglected and the sense of being discriminated against.

Jealousy occurs almost universally among children with the advent of a younger brother or sister who demands more attention from his parents, and gives an older child occasion to feel like a dethroned king. Those children become especially jealous who basked in the warm sunshine of their parents' love previous to the advent of the younger child. The case of a little girl who had committed three murders by the time she was eight years of age, shows to what lengths this feeling may go.

This little girl was a somewhat backward child who was prevented from doing any work because she was delicate. She found herself, consequently, in a relatively pleasant situation. This pleasant situation changed suddenly when she was six years old, and a sister arrived in the household. A total transformation took place in her soul, and she persecuted her younger sister with a ruthless hate. The parents, who could not understand her behavior, became strict, and attempted to show this child her responsibility for every misdeed. It happened that one day a little girl was found dead in the brook which passed by the village in which this family lived. Some time later another girl was found drowned, and finally our patient was caught just in the moment that she had thrown a third young child into the water. She admitted her murders, was put into an insane asylum for observation, and was finally placed in a sanatorium for further education.

In this case, the little girl's jealousy of her own sister was transferred to other young children. It was noticed that she had no hostile sentiments toward boys, and it seemed as though she saw the picture of her younger sister in these murdered children, and had attempted to satisfy her feeling of vengeance, for her neglect, in her murderous deeds.

Manifestations of jealousy can be produced even more easily when there are brothers and sisters. It is well known that in our civilization the fate of a girl child is not alluring; she can be easily discouraged when she sees her brother greeted more vociferously on his advent into the world, treated with greater care and respect, and allowed all manner of advantages from which a girl is excluded.

A relationship like this naturally gives rise to hostility. It may happen that an older sister will express her love, treat a younger brother like a mother, yet psychologically, this need not be different from the first case. If an older girl assumes the mother attitude to younger children, then she has regained a position of power where she can act and behave as she will; the trick enables her to create a valuable asset out of a dangerous position.

Exaggerated competition between brothers and sisters is one of the most frequent causes of family jealousy. A girl feels neglected, and drives unremittingly to overcome her brothers. Not infrequently, as a result of her industry and energy, she succeeds in outdistancing a brother, nature coming to her aid in the matter. A girl develops more quickly, both spiritually and physically, in her adolescence, than a boy, although this difference is slowly equalized in the course of the following years.

Jealousy has a thousand shapes. It may be recognized in mistrust and the preparation of ambushes for others, in the critical measurement of one's fellows, and in the constant fear of being neglected. Just which of these manifestations comes to the fore is dependent entirely upon the previous preparation for social life. One form of jealousy expresses itself in self-destruction, another expresses itself in energetic obstinacy. Spoiling the sport of others, senseless opposition, the restriction of another's freedom, and his consequent subjugation, are some of the protean shapes of this character trait.

Giving the other fellow a set of rules for his conduct is one favorite trick of jealousy. It is this characteristic psychic pattern along which an individual moves, when he attempts to foist certain laws of love upon his mate, when he builds a wall around his loved one, or prescribes where he should look, what he should do, and how he should think. Jealousy can also be put to the purpose of degrading and reproaching another; these are but means to an end: to rob another of his freedom of will, to set him in a rut, or to chain him down. A magnificent description of this type of behavior is to be found in Dostoyevsky's novel *Netotschka Njeswanowa*, in which a man succeds in oppressing his wife for her whole life, and thus expressing his dominance over her, by utilizing the trick we have just discussed. We see, therefore, that jealousy is an especially well-marked form of the striving for power.

III. Envy

Where there is a striving for power and domination, one can with certainty find the trait of envy in addition. The gulf between an individual and his supernaturally high goal expresses itself in the form of an inferiority complex. It oppresses him, and acquires such an influence upon his general behavior and his attitude toward life that one has the impression that he is a long way from his goal. His own

low evaluation of himself, and his constant dissatisfaction
with life are unfailing indicators thereof. He begins to spend
his time in measuring the success of others, in occupying
himself with what others think of him, or of what others
have accomplished. He is always the victim of a sense of
neglect, and he feels that discrimination has been exercised
against him. Such an individual may actually have more
than others. The various manifestations of this feeling of
being neglected are indices of an unsatisfied vanity, of a
desire to have more than one's neighbor, or indeed, to have
everything. Envious people of this type do not say that they
wish to have everything because the actual existence of a
social feeling prevents them from thinking these thoughts.
But they act *as if* they wanted to have everything.

The feeling of envy which grows up in the process of
this constant measuring of others' success does not lead
to greater possibilities of achieving happiness. The uni-
versality of the social feeling causes the universal dislike
of envy; yet there are but few who are not capable of some
envy. None of us is entirely free of it. In the even tenor of life
it may often not be evident, yet when a man suffers, or feels
himself oppressed, or lacks for money, food, dress, or warmth,
when his hope for the future is darkened, and he sees no
way out of his unfortunate situation, then envy appears.

We human beings stand today in the beginning of our
civilization. Although our ethics and our religion forbid
feelings of envy, we have not yet psychologically matured
enough to do without them. One can well understand the
envy of the impecunious. Such envy would be incomprehensible only if someone could prove that, placed in the
same position, he would not be envious. All that we wish
to say concerning this is that we must reckon with this
factor in the contemporary situation in the human soul.
The fact is that envy arises in the individual, or in the
group, as soon as one limits their activity too much. But
when envy appears in those most disagreeable forms which

we cannot ever approve, we do not actually know any means of obviating such envy and the frequently associated hate. One thing is clear to everyone who lives in our society, and that is that one should not put such tendencies to the test, nor provoke them; and that one should have sufficient tact not to accentuate any envious expressions which might be expected. Nothing is bettered by this course, it is true. Yet the very least we can demand of an individual is this: that he should not parade any temporary superiority over his fellows. He may too easily injure someone by the useless exhibition of his power.

The inseparable connection between the individual and society is indicated in the origin of this character trait. No one can lift himself above society, demonstrate his power over his fellows, without simultaneously arousing the opposition of others who want to prevent his success. Envy forces us to institute all those measures and rules whose purpose is the establishment of equality in all human beings. Finally we come rationally to a thesis which we have felt intuitively: *the law of the equality of all human beings.* This law may not be broken without immediately producing opposition and discord. It is one of the fundamental laws of human society.

The manifestations of envy are easily recognized, sometimes, indeed, in the very look of an individual. Envious traits which people have long used in their figures of speech have a physiological concomitant. One speaks of "green" or "pale" envy, pointing to the fact that envy influences the circulation of the blood. The organic expression of envy is found in the peripheral contraction of the capillary arteries.

So far as the pedagogic significance of envy is concerned, we have but one course. Since we cannot entirely destroy it, we must make it useful. This can be done by giving it a channel in which it can be made fruitful, without causing too great a shock to the psychic life. This holds good for the individual, as well as for a crowd. In the case of the individual we can prescribe an occupation which will elevate his self-esteem; in the life of nations, we can do nothing else than to show new ways to the development of innate, undeveloped powers to those nations which feel themselves neglected and watch their happier neighbors, fruitlessly envious of their better situation in the family of nations.

Anyone who has been envious all his life is useless for communal life. He will be interested solely in taking something away from another, in depriving him in some fashion, and in disturbing him. Simultaneously he will have the tendency to fix alibis for the goals which he has not attained, and blame others for his failures. He will be a fighter, a marplot, one who has no great love for good relationships, who has no part in the business of making himself useful to others. Since he hardly gives himself the trouble to sympathize with the situation of others, he has little understanding for human nature. He will not be moved by the fact that someone else suffers because of his actions. Envy may go so far as to lead a man to feel pleasure in the pain of his neighbor.

IV. Avarice

Avarice is closely related, and usually found, in the bad company of envy. By avarice we mean not only that form of greed which expresses itself in the hoarding of money, but also that more general form which expresses itself chiefly in that one is unable to give pleasure to another, that one is avaricious in his attitude toward society, and every other individual. The avaricious individual builds a wall about himself to be secure in the possession of his wretched treasures. On one hand, we recognize the connection with ambition and vanity, and on the other hand, the relationship to envy may be found. It is not an overstatement to say that all these character traits are usually present at the same time, and therefore, it is no astonishing trick of mind-reading, when one has discovered one of these traits, to declare that the others also are present.

Almost everyone in the civilization of today shows traces, at least, of avarice. The best the average man does is to veil it or hide it behind an exaggerated generosity, which is the equivalent of nothing more than the giving of alms, an attempt, through gestures of generosity, to elevate the personality-sense at the expense of others.

Under circumstances it would appear that avarice is actually a valuable quality, as when it is directed toward certain forms of life. One may be avaricious of one's time, or labor, and in the course of this actually do a great piece of work. There is a scientific and moral tendency in our present day which pushes this "time-greed" into the foreground, even demanding that everyone be economical of his time and labor. This sounds very well in theory, but wherever we see this thesis applied practically, we can always find that some individual goal of superiority and power is being served. This theoretically acquired thesis is frequently misused, the greed for time and labor is directed toward shifting the real burdens of work upon the shoulders of others. We can judge such activity, as all activity, only by the standard of its universal usefulness. It is a characteristic of the development of our technical age that human beings are treated as though they were machines, and that laws for life are given much as laws are given for technical activity. In the latter case such rules are often justified; but in the case of human beings they lead eventually to isolation, loneliness, and the destruction of human relationships. It will therefore be better to adjust our lives so that we would rather give, than save. This is a law which must not be taken from its context, with which one must not be allowed to practice mischief; with which one cannot, indeed, do mischief if one keeps the common weal in mind.

V. Hate

It is not seldom that we find hate as a characteristic of belligerent people. Tendencies to hate (which frequently appear early in childhood) may achieve a very high intensity, as in temper tantrums, while at the same time they appear in a milder form as nagging and maliciousness. The degree to which anyone is capable of hating and nagging is a good index of his personality. We know much about his soul when we have learned this fact, for hate and malice lend the personality a characteristic color.

Hate directs itself in various ways. It may be pointed towards various tasks which one must perform, against single individuals, against a nation, or a class, against a race or against the other sex. Hate does not appear openly, but like vanity, knows how to mask itself and appear, for instance, in the guise of a general critical attitude. Hate may expand itself in breaking all contact possibilities which an individual may have. Sometimes the degree to which an individual may hate is suddenly disclosed, as by a stroke of lightning. This occurred in the case of a patient who, himself exempted from war service, related how much he enjoyed reading the reports of the gruesome slaughter and destruction of others.

In crime we see much of this. In milder forms, hate tendencies may play a great rôle in our social life, appearing in forms which need not be at all insulting or horrifying. Misanthropy, that form of hate which betrays a very high degree of hostility to mankind, is one of these veiled forms. There are whole philosophical schools which are so permeated with hostility and misanthropy that they may be considered equivalent to coarser, undisguised hostile acts of cruelty and brutality. The veil is sometimes drawn aside in the biographies of famous men. It is less important to meditate on the inevitable truth of this statement than it is to remember that hate and cruelty may sometimes exist in an artist who ought to stand close to humanity if he wishes to create valid art.

The many ramifications of hate are to be found everywhere. If we do not examine them all here it is because it would take us too far afield to demonstrate all the relationships of single character traits to a general misanthropy. Certain occupations and professions, for instance, cannot be chosen without a certain misanthropic cast of mind. Grillparzer once said, "that a man's cruel instincts get a satisfying expression in his poetry." This by no means goes to say that these professions cannot be carried out without hate. Quite the contrary. In the very moment that an individual who is hostile to mankind decides to acquire an occupation, such as a military career, all his hostile tendencies are so directed that they fit, at least outwardly, into the social scheme. This happens as a result of the adjustment he must make to his organization, and because of the necessity of being connected with others who also have assumed this profession.

One form in which the hostile feelings are particularly well disguised are those actions which come under the head of "criminal negligence." "Criminal negligence" toward man or property is characterized by the fact that the negligent individual loses sight of all those considerations which the social feeling demands. The legal aspects of this question have caused unending discussion, but have never been entirely satisfactorily cleared up. It is self-understood that an action which might be termed "criminally negligent" is not identical with a crime. If we place a flower pot so close to the edge of a window that the slightest tremor might cause it to fall upon the head of some passerby, it is not the same as if we took this flower pot and actually threw it at someone. But the "criminally negligent" behavior of some individuals is unmistakably related to crime and is one other key to the understanding of human beings. In law, the fact that the "criminally negligent" act is not *consciously* intended is considered an extenuating circumstance, yet there is no doubt that an *unconsciously* hostile act is based upon the same degree of hostility as a consciously malicious deed. In observing the play of children one can always notice that certain children pay less attention to the welfare of others. We may be certain that they are not friendly toward their fellows. One should wait until one has further evidence to prove this fact, but if one finds that whenever these children are playing, some misfortune is sure to occur, we must admit that this child is unaccustomed to keep the welfare of his playfellows in mind.

At this point let us pay particular attention to our business life. Business is not especially adapted to convince us of the similarity between negligence and hostility. Business men have little concern for the welfare of competitors, or much interest in that social feeling which we consider so essential. A number of business procedures and enterprises are built clearly on the theory that the advantage of one business man can result only from the disadvantage of another. As a rule there is no punishment for such procedure even though there is a conscious malicious intention. These everyday business procedures in which there is a deficient social feeling, just as there is in "criminal negligence," poison our whole social life.

Even those who have the best of intentions, must, under the pressure of business, protect themselves as far as possible. We overlook the fact that this personal protection is usually accompanied by damage to someone else. We call attention to these matters because they explain the difficulty of exercising the social feeling under the pressure of business competition. Some solution must be found, so that cooperation of every individual toward the common weal will be made easier instead of more difficult, as is usually the case today. As a matter of fact the soul of mankind has been automatically at work attempting to effect a better order, in order to protect itself as best it may. Psychology must cooperate and set about understanding these changes to the end that it may not only understand business relationships, but also for the sake of understanding the psychic apparatus which plays its rôle at the same time. Only in this way can we know what may be expected of the individual and society.

Negligence is widespread in family, school, and life. We can find it in most of our institutions. Every now and again someone who does not consider his fellows in any way, finds his way into the head-lines. Naturally he does not go unpunished. The behavior of an inconsiderate human being usually ends unpleasantly for him. Sometimes this punishment follows only after many years. "The mills of the Gods grind slowly." It may be so long afterwards that the connection is not understood by one who has never tried to test his behavior with controls, who does not understand the relationship of cause and effect. Hence the complaints about an undeserved misfortune! The evil fate itself may be ascribed to the fact that others, who will no longer bear the inconsideration of their fellow, give up their personally well-intended efforts after a time, and withdraw themselves from his company.

Despite any apparent justification for criminally negligent deeds, it will be found on closer inspection, that they are the expressions of an essential misanthropy. For instance, a chauffeur who is driving over the speed limit, and has run over someone, will excuse himself by pleading an important appointment. We recognize in him a man whose petty personal affairs are placed above the welfare of his fellows, so that the dangers to which he exposes them are overlooked. The disparity between a man's personal affairs and the welfare of society gives us an index of his hostility to humanity.

CHAPTER III

NON-AGGRESSIVE CHARACTER TRAITS

Those character traits which are not openly hostile toward humanity, but give one the impression of a hostile *isolation*, may be grouped among the non-aggressive traits. It would seem as if the stream of hostility had been sidetracked. We have the impression of a psychic detour. Here we have the individual who never harms anyone, but withdraws from life and mankind, avoids all contact, and fails, because of his isolation, to cooperate with his fellows. The tasks of life, however, can be solved for the most part only in communal work. An individual who isolates himself may be suspected of the same hostility as one who wages open and direct warfare upon society. An enormous field of research discloses itself for our inspection and we shall demonstrate several of the outstanding manifestations more closely. The first trait which we must consider is timidity and seclusiveness.

I. Seclusiveness

Seclusiveness and isolation appear in a variety of forms. People who detach themselves from society speak little, or not at all, do not look their fellows in the eye, do not listen, or are inattentive when one speaks to them. In all social relations, even the simplest ones, they exhibit a certain frigidity which serves to separate them from their fellows. One feels this coldness in their manners and their deeds, in the way in which they shake hands, in the tone in which they speak, in the fashion with which they greet or refuse to greet others. They seem to be creating a distance between themselves and their fellows with every gesture.

In all these mechanisms of isolation we find an undercurrent of ambition and vanity. These people attempt to raise themselves above others by accentuating their differences from society. The most that they can win is an imaginary glory. A belligerent hostility is evident in the seemingly innocuous attitude of these exiles. Isolation may be a trait of larger groups. Everyone knows whole families whose life is hermetically sealed against approach from the outside. Their hostility, their conceit, and their belief that they are better and nobler than everyone else, is unmistakable. Isolation may be a trait of classes, religions, races, or nations, and it is sometimes an extraordinarily illuminating experience to walk through a strange town and see how, in the very structure of homes and dwellings, distinct social strata isolate themselves from others.

A deep-rooted trend of our culture allows human beings to isolate themselves into nations, creeds, and classes. Conflict, expressed in senile impotent traditions, is the sole result. It further enables some individuals to make use of latent contradictions, to set one group to fighting another, in order to satisfy their personal vanity. Such a class, or such an individual, considers itself especially excellent, values its spirit most highly, and occupies itself chiefly in demonstrating the evil of other people. The champions who work so hard to accentuate the difficulties between classes or nations, do so chiefly to heighten their personal vanity. If unfortunate events, such as a world war and its consequences, occur, they will be the last persons to take the blame for having started them. Hounded by their own insecurity, these troublemakers attempt to realize a sense of superiority and independence at the cost of others. Isolation is their sorry fate and their tiny cosmos. That they are

someone should turn on the lights, sit with him, play with him, and the like. So long as one obeys, his anxiety is dispelled, but the moment his sense of superiority is threatened, he becomes anxious again, and through his anxiety fortifies his commanding position.

There are similar phenomena in the life of grown-ups. There are individuals who do not like to go out alone. One can recognize them on the street because of their anxious gestures, and because of the anxious looks they cast about them. Some people will not move from one place to another, others seem to be running along the streets as if they were being pursued by an enemy. One is sometimes approached by a woman of this type who requests that one help her across the street. These are not weak, sick, invalids! They can walk quite easily, and are usually quite healthy, but in the face of an insignificant difficulty they are struck with anxiety and fear. Occasionally their anxiety and insecurity begin the very moment that they leave the house. Agoraphobia, or the fear of open places, is interesting for this reason. In the soul of sufferers from this symptom the feeling of being the victim of some hostile persecution is never dispelled. They believe that something differentiates them entirely from other people. Fear that they might fall (which means nothing more to us than that they feel themselves very greatly elevated) is an expression of their attitude. In the pathological forms of fear, the same goal of power and superiority may be seen. For many people anxiety is an obvious device to compel someone to be close to them, and occupy themselves with the person of the sufferer. Under such circumstances we see that no one can leave the room lest the sufferer become anxious again! Everyone must subjugate himself to the patient's anxiety. The anxiety of one person thus imposes a law upon the whole environment. Everyone must come to the patient, while the patient need go to no one. He becomes the king who rules everyone else.

Fear of human beings can be dissolved solely by that

bond which binds the individual to humanity. Only that individual can go through life without anxiety who is conscious of belonging to the fellowship of man.

Timidity is a milder if not less noteworthy form of anxiety. What we have said of anxiety holds equally for timidity. Let the relationships in which children are placed be as simple as you will, timidity will always allow them to avoid contacts, or break them when they are made. The feeling of inferiority, and the sense of being different from others, inhibits these children from finding any joy in making new contacts.

III. Faint-heartedness

Faint-heartedness is a characteristic of those who feel that every task which faces them is especially difficult; of people who have no confidence in their powers to accomplish anything. As a rule this trait is evinced in the form of slowed movements. Thus the distance between the individual and his approaching test or task, not only does not quickly become smaller, but may even remain unchanged. People who are always to be found elsewhere when they should be applying themselves to some particular problem of life, belong to this group. Such individuals suddenly discover that they are not at all fit for the profession which they have chosen, or they find all manner of objections which serve so to annihilate their sense of logic, that the assumption of this profession actually becomes impossible. Besides slowed movements, the expression of faint-heartedness is to be found in a certain preoccupation with over-safety and over-preparation, activities which have for their sole purpose the evasion of all responsibility.

Individual Psychology has called the complex of questions applicable to this extraordinarily wide-spread phenomenon, "the problem of distance." It has created a standpoint from which we can inexorably judge a human being and measure his distance from the solution of the three great problems of life. These problems are: the solution of the question of his social responsibilities, the relationship between the "I" and the "you," the question whether he has fostered his contact between himself and his fellows in an approximately correct manner, or has hindered this contact. The other questions and problems are the problem of profession and occupation, and the problem of love and marriage. From the degree of failure, from the distance of an individual from the solution of these problems, we may draw far-reaching conclusions as to his personality. At the same time we can use the data which we have gathered in this manner, to aid us in our understanding of human nature.

In cases of faint-heartedness, such as those we have indicated, the basis may be found in the desire of an individual to separate himself from his tasks by a greater or lesser distance. There is, however, a bright side next to the dark pessimism which we have described. We may assume that our patient has chosen his position entirely because of this brighter side. If he approaches a task entirely unprepared for it, then there are extenuating circumstances if he should fail, and his personality-sense and vanity remain untouched. The situation becomes much more secure, and he acts like a tight-rope walker who knows there is a net beneath him. If he falls, he falls softly, and if he approaches a job unprepared for it and fails, his sense of personal value is not in danger because he can say that a variety of causes have prevented a full performance. Had he not started too late, or had he been better prepared, success would have been certain. In this way it is not a defect of the personality which is at fault, but some petty circumstance for which he cannot be expected to assume responsibility. If he should succeed, his success is the more brilliant. For if someone performs his duties industriously, no one is surprised if he accomplishes his end, as his success seems self-understood.

If, on the other hand, he begins too late, works but a little, or is quite unprepared, and still solves his problem, he then appears in quite another light. He becomes, so to speak, a double hero who has done with one hand what others can do only with two hands!

These are the advantages of psychic détours. Yet the détour attitude betrays not only ambition, but also vanity, and points to the fact that an individual likes to play a heroic role, at least for himself. All his activity is directed toward personal inflation, so that he may have the semblance of particular powers.

Society has no place for deserters. A certain adaptability and subordination are necessary to play the game, to be helpful, not to assume leadership simply for the purpose of ruling. The truth of this law, many of us have observed in ourselves, or in others in our environment. We know individuals who may pay visits, behave themselves well, who do not disturb others, but are not able to be warm friends because their striving for power prevents them. It is not strange that others cannot become warm toward them. An individual of this class will sit quietly at a table, and not show the outer aspects of a happily constituted human being. He will prefer a dialogue to an open discussion, and will show his true character in insignificant things. He will for instance go to great lengths to prove himself right, even when his rightness is of little concern to others. It will soon be seen that the argument itself is of little value to him so long as he is proven in the right, and others in the wrong. Again, at the point of détour, he shows puzzling manifestations, becomes tired without knowing why, gets into a hurry which never brings him forward, cannot sleep, loses his powers, has all kinds of complaints. In short we hear nothing from him but complaints for which he can give no adequate reasons. He seems to be a sick man, he is "nervous."

In actuality all these are crafty devices for diverting his

attention from the indicators that point out the true state of affairs which he fears. It is no accident that he has chosen these weapons. Think of the stubborn rebelliousness of a man who is afraid of that universal phenomenon, night! We can rest assured, when we see such a one, that he has never been reconciled with the business of living on this earth. Nothing else would satisfy his ego but to do away with night! He demands this as a set condition of his adjustment to a normal life. But by setting this impossible condition he betrays his bad intentions! He is a no-sayer to life!

All nervous manifestations of this sort originate at that point where the nervous individual becomes frightened of the problems he must solve, and what are they but these necessary duties and obligations of every-day life? When these appear on the horizon he looks for an excuse, either to approach them more slowly, or under extenuating circumstances, or he seeks an alibi for avoiding them entirely. In this way he simultaneously avoids those obligations which are necessary for the maintenance of human society, and injures not only his immediate environment, but, in larger relationships, everyone else. If we understood human nature better, and were in a position to keep in mind that terrible causality which effects these tragic results at some distant time, we might long ago have made such symptoms impossible. It does not pay to attack the logical and immanent laws of human society. Because of the long time element, and the innumerable complications which may occur, we are seldom enabled to fix these connections between crime and retribution exactly, and draw illuminating conclusions from them. Only when we allow a whole life's behavior pattern to unfold before us, and intensively study the history of a human being, are we able, with much care, to gain insight into these connections, and to demonstrate where the original mistake was made.

IV. Untamed Instincts as the Expression of Lessened Adaptation

There are people who show a character trait which we might call uncouthness or lack of civilization to a remarkable degree. Those who bite their nails, or constantly pick their noses, and others who throw themselves upon food so that their behavior gives the impression of an untamed passion for eating, belong in this class. That these manifestations are significant is clear the minute that we watch such an individual who approaches his meals like a hungry wolf, and knows no inhibition nor shame in expressing his greed. What noisy eating! The biggest bites disappear into the abyss of his maw! What remarkable speed in eating! How much he eats! And how often! Has not everyone seen individuals who are not happy if they are not always eating something?

Another manifestation of uncouthness is dirtiness and disorderliness. The lack of formality of people who have much work to do, or the natural disorder which one can occasionally find when a man is hard at work, is not meant here. The type referred to usually does not work, usually remains far from all useful work, yet will never be free of external disorder and filth. These are individuals who seem to seek dilapidation and offensiveness, and we could not imagine them without their characteristic trait.

These are but some of the external characteristics of an uncouth human being. They clearly show us that he is not playing the game, and wants really, to remove himself from other human beings. People who commit these and other uncouth acts lead us to believe that they have little use for their fellows. Most uncouthnesses begin in childhood, for hardly any children develop in a straight-away line, but there are grown-ups who have never overcome these childish traits.

At the basis of these manifestations is a more or less well-marked disinclination of these uncouth people to meet with their fellow-men. Every uncouth individual wishes to hold himself distant from life, and is disinclined to co-operate. That they are not amenable to moralizing preachments to give up their uncouthness is easily comprehensible, for when one is disinclined to play the game of life according to the rules, he is, as a matter of fact, quite right in biting his nails or in exhibiting some similar trait. There is really hardly a better way of avoiding human beings, no more effective means to this end, than to appear always in a dirty collar, or in a spotted suit. What could prevent him more absolutely from holding a position in which he is subject to criticism and competition and the attention of others, or what would be more favorable in his retreat from love or marriage, than if he would appear always in this fashion? He loses out in the competition as a matter of course, and at the same time he has an actual excuse in that he always blames it on his uncouthness, "What couldn't I do if I didn't have this bad habit!" he exclaims, but in an aside he whispers his alibi, "Unfortunately, I have it, however!"

Let us show one case in which a barbarism became an instrument of self defense and was used in order to tyrannize the environment. It is the case of a twenty-two-year-old girl who was a bed-wetter. She was the next to the last child in her family, and because of the fact that she was a weak and sickly child enjoyed the particular solicitude of her mother, on whom she was exceptionally dependent. She managed to chain her mother to her by day and by night, by means of anxiety states during the day, and night terrors and bed-wetting, at night. In its beginning this must have been a triumph for her, a balsam for her vanity. She succeeded in retaining her mother for herself, by means of her misbehavior, at the expense of her brothers and sisters.

This girl was exceptional also in that she could not be

moved to make friends, go into society, nor attend school. She was particularly anxious when she had to leave the house, and even when she grew older, and had to run errands in the evening, walking alone at night was agony for her. She came home thoroughly fatigued and anxious, and told all manner of terrible stories of the dangers which she had run. We can see how all these traits signified only that this young woman wanted to remain constantly at her mother's side, but since financial circumstances would not allow this, an occupation had to be found for her. She was finally almost driven to take a position, but after two brief days, her old disease, bed-wetting, returned, forced her to give up her position because her employers were incensed at her. Her mother who did not understand the true meaning of her illness, reproached her bitterly. The young woman then attempted suicide, and was taken to a hospital; and now her mother swore to her that she would never leave her again.

All these things, the bed-wetting, fear of the night, her fear of being alone, and her attempted suicide, were directed toward the same goal. For us they mean: "I must remain close to my mother, or, mother must pay constant attention to me!" In this way an uncouthness, the habit of bed-wetting, acquires a valid meaning. Now we can recognize that a human being may be judged according to such bad habits. At the same time we know that these mistakes can be removed only when we understand the patient entirely, and according to his context.

By and large, we shall usually find childish barbarisms and bad habits are directed toward acquiring the attention of the adult environment. Children who want to play a grand rôle, or show their grown-ups how weak and incapable they are, will make use of them. The common trait of behaving very badly while visiting strangers are present, has a similar meaning. The best-behaved children sometimes seem to be possessed of the devil as soon as a guest enters the house. The child wants to play a rôle and does not stop his attempts to do so until his purpose has been gained in some manner which seems satisfactory to him. When such children grow up they will attempt to evade the demands of society by some such barbarisms, or they will attempt to frustrate the common weal by making it difficult for others to get along. An imperious, ambitious vanity is hidden beneath all such manifestations. Only the fact that these manifestations are varied and well disguised prevents us from recognizing clearly what their cause is, and to what end they are directed.

CHAPTER IV

OTHER EXPRESSIONS OF CHARACTER

1. Cheerfulness

We have already drawn attention to the fact that we can easily measure anyone's social feeling by learning to what degree he is prepared to serve, to help, and to give pleasure to others. The talent for bringing pleasure to others makes a man more interesting. Happy people approach us more easily and we judge them emotionally as being more sympathetic. It seems that we sense these traits as indicators of a highly developed social feeling, quite instinctively. There are people who appear cheerful, who do not go about forever oppressed and solicitous, who do not unload their worries upon every stranger. They are quite capable, when in the company of others, to radiate this cheerfulness and make life more beautiful and meaningful. One can sense that they are good human beings, not only in their actions, but in the manner in which they approach, in which they speak, in which they pay attention to our interests, as well as in their entire external aspect, their clothes, their gestures, their happy emotional state, and in their laughter. That far-seeing psychologist, Dostoyevsky, has said that "One can recognize a person's character much better by his laughter than by a boring psychological examination." Laughter can make connections as well as break them. We have all heard the aggressive notes of those who laugh at others' misfortune. There are some people who are absolutely unable to laugh because they stand so far from the innate bond which connects human beings, that their ability to give pleasure or to appear happy, is absent. That there is another little group of people who are utterly incapable of giving anyone else

joy since they are concerned only in embittering life in every
situation which they may enter. They walk around as though
they wished to extinguish every light. They do not laugh
at all, or only when forced to do so, or when they wish to
give the semblance of being a joy-giver. The mystery of the
emotions of sympathy and antipathy are thus made understandable.

The opposite of the sympathetic type occurs in those who
are chronic kill-joys and marplots. They advertise the world
as a vale of sorrow and pain. Some individuals go through
life as though they were bent by the weight of a great load.
Every little difficulty is exploited, the future appears black
and depressing, and they do not miss an occasion in which
others are happy, to utter doleful Cassandra-like prophecies.
They are pessimistic in every fibre, not only for themselves
but for everyone else. If someone is happy in their neighborhood they become restless and attempt to find some gloomy
aspect to the event. This they do, not only with their words,
but with their disturbing actions, in this way preventing
others from living happily and enjoying their fellowship in
humanity.

II. Thought Processes and Ways of Expression

The thought processes and manner of expression of some
individuals sometimes makes so plastic an impression that
we cannot help being aware of it. Some people think and
speak as though their mental horizon was circumscribed
by mottoes and proverbs. One can tell in advance what they
will say. They sound like cheap novels, and they speak in
catch-word phrases taken from the worst newspapers. Their
speech is full of slang or technical expressions. This type
of expression may well give us a further understanding of a
human being. There are thoughts and words which one does
not, or may not, use. Their vulgar and coarse style reëchoes

in every sentence and sometimes frightens even the speaker himself. It bears witness to the speaker's lack of empathy in judgment and critique of others, when he answers every question with a catch-word phrase, or a slang expression, and thinks and acts according to the clichés of the tabloids and the movies. Needless to say there are many people who cannot think in any other way, and in this way, give evidence of their psychic retardation.

III. School-boy Immaturity

Frequently we meet people who give the impression that they have stopped their development somewhere in their school career and have never been able to grow beyond the "prep-school" stage. At home, at work, and in society, they act like school-boys, eagerly listening and waiting for a chance to say something. They are always anxious to answer any question which is asked at a gathering, as though they wanted to be quite sure that everyone knew that they also knew something about the subject, and were waiting for a good school report to prove it. The key to these people is the fact that they feel safety only in definite fixed forms of life. They are anxious and insecure whenever they find themselves in a situation in which a school-boy behavior would be inadequate. This trait appears at various intellectual levels. In less sympathetic cases the individual appears dry, sober, and unapproachable, or attempts to play the rôle of the man who knows every subject from its basic principles, who either knows everything immediately, or seeks to catalogue it according to predetermined rules and formulæ.

IV. Pedants and Men of Principle

An interesting example of this scholastic type is to be found in the people who attempt to pigeon-hole every activity and every event according to some principle which they have assumed valid for every situation. They believe in this principle and they are not to be brought to relinquish it, nor would they be comfortable if everything could not be interpreted according to it. They are the dry-as-dust pedants. We have the impression that they feel themselves so insecure that they must squeeze all of life and living into a few rules and formulæ, lest they become too frightened of it. Faced with a situation for which they have no rule or formulæ, they can only run away. They are insulted and displeased if anyone plays a game in which they are not versed. It goes without saying that one can exercise a great deal of power by the use of this method. Think for instance of the innumerable cases of unsocial "conscientious objectors." We know that these overconscientious individuals are moved by an unchecked vanity and a boundless desire to rule.

Even if they are good workers, their dry-as-dust pedantic attitude is obvious. They show no initiative, become narrowly circumscribed in their interests, and are full of their fads and whimsicalities. They may develop the habit of always walking on the outside of a stair, for example, or walk only on the cracks in the pavement. Others cannot be brought to forsake an accustomed path at any cost. All these types have not much sympathy for the real things of life. In working out their principles they waste an enormous amount of time, and sooner or later, get perfectly out of tune both with themselves and with their environment. In the moment in which a new situation to which they are not accustomed occurs, they fail entirely because they are not prepared to solve it, because they believe that without rules and magic formulæ nothing can be done. They will religiously avoid all change. It will be difficult for them, for instance, to accustom themselves to springtime because they have so long adjusted themselves to winter. The road into the open which appears with the warmer season arouses the fear in them that they will have to make more contacts with other humans, and they feel badly as a result. These are the individuals who complain that they feel worse in the Spring. Since they can adjust themselves to new situations only with the greatest difficulty, we will find them in positions which demand little initiative. No employer would place them in any other position as long as they have not changed themselves. These are no hereditary traits, no unchangeable manifestations, but a mistaken attitude toward life, which has taken possession of their souls with such power that it entirely dominates their personality. In the end the individual cannot free himself from his ingrown prejudices.

V. Submissiveness

People who are permeated by a spirit of servility are likewise not well adapted to positions which demand initiative. They are comfortable when they are obeying someone else's commands. The servile individual lives by the rules and laws of others, and this type seeks out a servile position almost compulsively. This servile attitude is found in the most varied of life's relationships. One can surmise its existence in the outer carriage, which usually is a somewhat bent and cringing attitude. We see them bending themselves in the presence of others, listening carefully to everyone's words, not so much to weigh and consider them, but rather to carry out their commands, and to echo and reaffirm their sentiments. They consider it an honor to appear submissive, sometimes to a perfectly unbelievable degree.

There are people who find a real pleasure in subjugating themselves. Far be it from us to say that those who wish to dominate at all times are an ideal type, yet we wish to show the darker side of the life of those who find a true solution of their life's problems in submission.

It may be said that there are many for whom submission is a law of life. We do not refer to the servant classes. We are speaking of the female sex. That woman must be submissive, is an unwritten but deeply rooted law to which a number of people subscribe as to a fixed dogma. They believe that women are here only for the purpose of being submissive. These are ideas which have poisoned and destroyed all human relationships, yet this superstition cannot be weeded out. There are, even among women, many believers, who feel that it is an eternal law they must obey. But no one has ever seen a case where anyone has gained anything by such a viewpoint. Sooner or later someone complains that if a woman had not been so submissive everything would have turned out better.

Quite apart from the fact that the human soul will not bear submission without revolt, a submissive woman sooner or later becomes dependent, and socially sterile, as the following case will show. This was a woman who married a famous man for love. Both she and her husband subscribed to the above-mentioned dogma. In time she had become simply a machine for which there was nothing but duty, service, and more service. Every independent gesture vanished from her life. Her environment had become accustomed to her submission, and did not object especially, but no one profited by this silence.

This case did not degenerate into greater difficulties because it occurred among relatively cultured people. But let us consider that in a large portion of mankind the submission of woman is her self-understood destiny, so that we may realize how much cause for conflict lies in this view. When a husband considers this submission as a matter of course, he may take offense at any moment, because actually such submission is impossible.

Women are to be found who are so permeated with the spirit of submission that they seek out the very men who appear imperious or brutal. Sooner or later this unnatural relationship degenerates into open war. One sometimes has the impression that these women want to make the submission of women appear ridiculous, and prove that it is folly!

We have already learned a way out of these difficulties. When a man and woman live together, they must live under the conditions of a comradely division of labor in which neither one nor the other is subjugated. If, for the time being, this is but an ideal, at least it gives us a standard to measure the cultural advance of an individual. The question of submission not only plays a rôle in the relationship of the sexes and burdens the masculine sex with a thousand difficulties which it is incapable of ever solving, but it also plays an important rôle in the life of nations.

The ancient civilization built up their whole economic situation on the institution of slavery. Perhaps the greatest number of people who are alive today originated in slave families, and hundreds of years have passed during which two classes of people lived in absolute strangeness and opposition to each other. Today, indeed, among certain people the caste system is still retained, and the principle of submission and the slavery of one to another exists, and may at any time give rise to a definite type of man. In the ancient days it was customary to believe that work was the relatively degrading occupation of slaves and that the master did not dirty himself with common labors, that he was not only the commander, but that all worthwhile traits were united in his character. The ruling class consisted of the "best" and the Greek word "Aristos" signifies this. Aristocracy was domination by the "best," but this "best" was determined entirely by power, not by the examination of

virtues and qualities. Examination and classification occurred only among the slaves. The aristocrat was he who
held the power.

In modern times our point of view has been influenced
by the previous existence of slavery and aristocracy. The
necessity of bringing human beings closer has robbed these
institutions of all meaning and significance. The great
thinker, Nietzsche, advocated rule by the best, and subjugation of everyone else. It is difficult today to exclude from
our thought processes the division of human beings into
master and servant, and to consider everyone as quite equal.
Yet the mere possession of the new point of view of the
absolute equality of every human being, is a step in advance,
adapted to help us, and prevent us from falling into considerable errors in our conduct. There are human beings
who have become so servile that they are happy only when
they can be thankful to someone else. They are forever
excusing themselves, seemingly for their very existence in
the world. We must not be deceived into believing that they
do this gladly. For the most part they feel themselves very
unhappy.

VI. Imperiousness

Contrasted to the servile individual we have just described, is the imperious individual who must have a
dominant rôle, and is anxious to play the chief part. He
is concerned with but one question in all life, "How can I
be superior to everyone?" This rôle carries all manner of
disappointments with it. To a certain degree the imperious
rôle may be useful, if it is not accompanied by too much
hostile aggression and activity. Wherever a director is necessary you will find one of these imperiously-minded individuals. They seek out positions where commands and organization are of advantage. In times of unrest, when a nation

is in revolution, such natures come to the surface, and it is quite understandable that just such individuals should appear, for they have the proper gestures, the proper attitudes and desires, and usually also the necessary preparation to assume the leader's rôle. They have been accustomed to commanding in their own homes. No game satisfies them unless they can play the king, the ruler, or the general. Among them are individuals who are incapable of the least performance, if someone else is dictating; they become excited and anxious as soon as they must obey another's command. In quiet times, one finds such individuals heading small groups, whether in business or in society. They are always in the foreground because they push themselves, and have much to say. So long as they do not disturb the rules of the game of life, we can have no objection to them, despite the fact that we cannot subscribe to the over-evaluation of such individuals which society holds today. They too are but human beings who stand before an abyss, for they cannot play well in the rank and file, they do not make the best of team-mates. All their life they strain themselves to the uttermost, never acquiring any ease until they have proven their superiority in some way.

VII. Mood and Temperament

Psychology is mistaken if it believes that those human beings whose attitude to life and its tasks are very dependent upon their mood or temperament, owe this quality to their heredity. Mood and temperament are not inherited. They occur in overly ambitious, and therefore hypersensitive, natures whose dissatisfaction with life expresses itself in various evasions. Their hypersensitivity is like an outstretched feeler with which they test every new situation before they make a final approach to it.

It would seem, however, that there are some people who

are always in a cheerful mood. They go to great lengths to create a happy atmosphere as a necessary basis of their life, laying stress upon its brighter side. We can find all variations of level among them. There are some among them who are childishly jolly, and have something very touching in their childishness. They approach their tasks not by evasion, but in a certain playful, childish way and solve them as though they were games or puzzles. There is perhaps no type which is more sympathetic and beautiful in its attitude.

But among them there are some who carry their cheerfulness too far, who approach situations which are relatively serious, in the same childish manner. Sometimes this is so inappropriate to the earnestness of life, that we get bad impressions. One feels uncertain, seeing them at work, getting an impression that they are really irresponsible, because they wish to overcome difficulties too easily. As a result, they are kept from the really difficult tasks, which they usually avoid of their own accord. Yet we cannot take leave of this type without paying a certain tribute to it. This type is always pleasant to work with. It forms a pleasant contrast to those other types which go about with gloomy faces. Cheerful people can be won over much more easily than pessimists, who proceed in a sad and discontented way, finding only the dark side of every situation which they meet.

VIII. Hard Luck

It is a psychological truism that whoever gets into difficulties with the absolute truth and logic of communal life, will sooner or later feel the repercussion somewhere in the course of his existence. As a rule the individuals who make these profound mistakes do not learn from experience, but consider their misfortune as an unjustified personal mishap

which has fallen upon them. It takes them their whole life
to demonstrate what hard luck they have had, and prove
that they have never succeeded in anything, because everything that they have laid their hands upon has ended in
failure. One even finds the tendency on the part of these
unfortunates to be proud of their ill-luck, as though some
supernatural power had caused it. Examine this point of
view more closely and you will find that vanity is again
playing its evil game here. They are the individuals who act
as though some sinister deity spent its time persecuting
them. In a thunder storm they believe that the lightning will
single them out. They are afraid that burglars will enter their
particular house. If any misfortune is to occur they are
certain that they are the ones it will touch.

Only a man who considers himself the center of all events
can exaggerate like this. It seems very modest to be constantly pursued by misfortune, but actually a stubborn
vanity is at work when such individuals feel that all hostile
powers are concerned with reeking vengeance upon them.
They are the individuals who embittered their childhood
by believing themselves the prey of robbers, murderers, and
other unpleasant gentry, such as ghosts and spirits, as
though all these individuals and apparitions had nothing
more to do than persecute them.

It is to be expected that their attitude will be expressed
in their external carriage. They walk as though under
pressure, bent over so that no one can mistake the heavy
load under which they move. They remind us of those
Karyatids who supported the Greek temples, and spent
their whole lives holding up porticos. They take everything
more than seriously, and judge everything pessimistically.
It is not hard to understand why things always go wrong
for them. They are persecuted by ill luck because they not
only embitter their own lives but also those of others.
Vanity is at the root of their misfortune. Being unlucky is
one way of being important!

IX. Religiosity

Some of these chronically misunderstood people beat a retreat into religion, where they proceed to do just what they have done before. They complain and commiserate with themselves, and shift their pains upon the shoulders of a complacent God. Their whole activity concerns itself solely with their own person. In this process they believe that God, this extraordinarily honored and worshipped Being, is concerned entirely with serving them, and is responsible for their every action. In their opinion He may be brought into even closer connection by artificial means, as by some particularly zealous prayer, or other religious rites. In short, the dear God knows nothing else and has nothing else to do, but to occupy Himself with their troubles, and pay a great deal of attention to them. There is so much heresy in this type of religious worship that if the old days of Inquisition were to return, these very religious fanatics would probably be the first to be burned. They approach their God just as they approach their fellowmen, complainingly, whining, yet never lifting a hand to help themselves or better their circumstances. Cooperation, they feel, is an obligation only for others.

The history of an eighteen-year-old girl demonstrates the extent to which this vain egoism may go. She was a very good and industrious, though very ambitious child. Her ambition expressed itself in her religion, in which she performed every rite with the utmost piety. One day she began to reproach herself for having been too unorthodox in her belief, and having broken the commandments, and for having held sinful thoughts from time to time. The result was that she spent the whole day violently accusing herself, with such vehemence that everyone felt that she had become insane. She spent the day kneeling in a corner, bitterly reproaching herself; yet no one else could reproach her for a single thing. One day a priest tried to remove the burden of her sin by explaining to her that she had really never sinned, and that her salvation was certain. The next day this young girl planted herself before him on the street, and screamed at him that he was unworthy of entering a church because he had taken such a burden of sin upon his shoulders. We need not discuss this case further, but it illustrates how ambition breaks into religious problems, and how vanity makes its bearer a judge over virtue, vice, purity, corruption, good, and evil.

CHAPTER V

AFFECTS AND EMOTIONS

Affects and emotions are accentuations of what we have previously designated as character traits. Emotions express themselves as a sudden discharge (under the pressure of some conscious or unconscious necessity) and like character traits, they have a definite goal and direction. We might call them psychic movements which possess a definite time boundary. The affects are not mysterious phenomena which defy interpretation; they occur wherever they are appropriate to the given style of life and the predetermined behavior pattern of the individual. Their purpose is to modify the situation of the individual in whom they occur, to his benefit. They are the accentuated, more vehement, movements which occur in an individual who has foregone other mechanisms for achieving his purpose, or has lost faith in any other possibilities of attaining his goal.

We are dealing again with the individual who, burdened by a feeling of inferiority and inadequacy which forces him to gather all his powers together and exert greater efforts, makes more drastic movements than would otherwise be necessary. By dint of these more strenuous efforts he believes it possible to bring his person into the limelight, and prove himself victorious. Just as we cannot have anger without an enemy, we cannot conceive of the emotion of anger without considering also that its purpose is a victory over this enemy. In our culture it is still possible to achieve one's ends by means of these accentuated movements. We should have fewer outbursts of temper if there were no possibility of attaining recognition by this method.

Individuals who do not have sufficient confidence in their ability to achieve their goal, do not give up their purpose because of their feeling of insecurity, but attempt to approach it by dint of greater efforts, and with the aid of accessory affects and emotions. It is a method by which an individual, stung by a sense of his inferiority, gathers his powers together and attempts to win a desired objective in the manner of some brutal uncivilized savage.

Since the affects and emotions are closely bound up with the very essence of personality, they are not solitary characteristics of solitary individuals, but are to be found more or less regularly among all people. Every individual is capable of showing some particular emotion if he is brought into the proper situation. We might call this the faculty for emotion.[1] The emotions are so essentially a part of human life that we are all capable of experiencing them. So soon as we have gained a fairly deep knowledge of a human being we may well be able to imagine his usual affects and emotions, without ever having actually come into contact with them. It is quite natural that so deeply rooted a phenomenon as an affect or an emotion, shows its effect upon the body, since body and soul are so intimately alloyed. The physical phenomena which accompany the presence of affects and emotions are indicated by various changes in the blood vessels and in the respiratory apparatus, as in the appearance of blushing, pallor, rapid pulse, and variations of the respiratory rate.

I. Disjunctive Affects

A. ANGER

Anger is an affect which is the veritable epitome of the striving for power and domination. This emotion betrays very clearly that its purpose is the rapid and forceful

[1] Translator's note: In the original, the word Affektbereitschaft is used. There is no adequate English translation for this word,

destruction of every obstacle in the way of its angry bearer. Previous researches have taught us that an angry individual is one who is striving for superiority by the strenuous application of all his powers. The striving for recognition occasionally degenerates into a veritable power-intoxication. Where this occurs we are prepared to find individuals who respond to the least stimulus which might detract from their sense of power, with paroxysms of anger. They believe (perhaps as a result of previous experiences) that they can most easily have their own way, and conquer their opponents, by this mechanism. This method does not stand upon a very high intellectual level, yet it works in a majority of cases. It is not difficult for most people to remember how they have rewon their prestige through an occasional outburst of fury.

There are occasions when anger is largely justified, but we are not considering these cases here. When we speak of anger we speak of individuals in whom this affect is ever present, and is a habitual, well-marked response. Some people actually make a system out of their anger and are notable because they have no other way to approach a problem. They are usually haughty, highly sensitive people who cannot brook a superior or an equal, who must themselves be superior to be happy. Consequently their eyes are sharpened, and they are continually on guard lest someone should approach them too closely, or does not value them highly enough. Distrust is a character trait which is most frequently allied with their sensitivity. They find it impossible to trust a fellow human being.

Other character traits which are closely related will be found concomitant with their anger, their sensitivity, and their mistrust. In the difficult cases it is quite possible to conceive such an exceptionally ambitious individual fright-

---

which denotes a lability of the soul; that is to say, that the soul possesses the possibility of effecting new emotional constellations appropriate to any given new situation.

ened from every serious task, and thus incapable of ever adjusting himself to society. Should he be denied anything, he knows but one method of response. He announces his protest in a manner which is usually very painful to his environment. He may for instance shatter a mirror, or destroy a costly vase. One cannot well believe him if he attempts, afterwards, to excuse himself by saying that he did not know what he was doing. The desire to injure his environment is too plainly evident, for he will always destroy something valuable, and never confine his rage to worthless objects. A plan must have been present in his action.

Albeit in smaller circles this method achieves a certain success, so soon as the circle becomes larger it loses its effectiveness. These habitually angry people therefore are soon to be found in conflict with the world all along the line.

The external attitude which accompanies the affect of anger is so common that we have but to mention fury to imagine the picture of an irascible man. The hostile attitude towards the world is clearly evident. The affect of anger signifies an almost complete negation of the social feeling. The striving for power is so bitterly expressed that the death of an opponent becomes easily conceivable. We can practice our knowledge of human nature by solving the various emotions and affects which we observe, since affects and emotions are the clearest indications of character. We must designate all irascible, angry, acrimonious individuals as enemies of society, and enemies of life. We must again call attention to the fact that their striving for power is built upon the foundations of their feeling of inferiority. No human being who realizes his own power is under the necessity of showing these aggressive, violent movements and gestures. This fact must never be overlooked. In paroxysms of rage, the whole gamut of inferiority and superiority appears with utter clarity. It is a cheap trick whereby the personal evaluation is raised at the cost of another's misfortune.

Alcohol is one of the most important factors which facilitate the appearance of rage and anger. Very small quantities of alcohol are often sufficient to produce this effect. It is well known that the action of alcohol deadens or removes the civilized inhibitions. An intoxicated person acts as if he had never been civilized. In this way he loses control of himself, and consideration for others. When he is not intoxicated he may be able to hide his hostility to mankind and inhibit his inimical tendencies at the cost of great efforts. Once he is intoxicated his true character is expressed. It is by no means a fortuitous circumstance that those individuals who are out of harmony with life are the first to take to alcohol. They find in the drug a certain consolation and forgetfulness, as well as an excuse for the fact that they have not attained what they desire.

Temper tantrums are much more frequent among children than among adults. Sometimes an insignificant event is sufficient to throw a child into temper tantrums. This arises from the fact that children, as a result of their greater feeling of inferiority, show their striving for power in a more transparent manner. An angry child is striving for recognition. Every obstacle he meets appears exceptionally difficult, if not insurmountable.

The results of anger, when they go beyond the usual context of swearing and rage, may actually injure the person who is angry. We may well write a note in this connection, on the nature of suicide. In suicide we see the attempt to injure relatives or friends, and revenge oneself for some defeat which has been suffered.

B. SADNESS

The affect of sadness occurs when one cannot console himself for a loss or deprivation. Sadness, along with the other affects, is a compensation for a feeling of displeasure or weakness, and amounts to an attempt to secure a better situation. In this respect its value is identical with that of a temper paroxysm. The difference is that it occurs as a result of other stimuli, is marked by a different attitude, and utilizes a different method. The striving for superiority is present, just as in all other affects, whereas an irate individual seeks to elevate his self-evaluation and degrade his opponent, and his anger is directed against an opponent. Sadness amounts to an actual shrinkage of the psychic front, which is a prerequisite to the subsequent expansion in which the sad individual achieves his personal elevation and satisfaction. But this satisfaction exists as a kind of discharge, a movement which is directed against the environment, although in a different manner than in the case of anger. The sad person complains and with his complaint sets himself into opposition to his fellows. Natural as sorrow is in the nature of man, its exaggeration is a hostile gesture against society.

The elevation of the sorrower is attained consequent to the attitude of his environment. We all know how sorrowing individuals find their position made easier by the fact that others place themselves in their service, sympathize with them, support them, encourage them, or contribute tangibly to their welfare. If the psychic discharge succeeds as a result of tears and loud sorrow, it is evident that the sorrower achieves his elevation over his environment by making himself a judge and critic, or a plaintiff, against the existing order of things. The more the plaintiff demands of his environment because of his sorrow, the more transparent his claims become. Sadness becomes an irrefutable argument which places a binding duty upon the sorrower's neighbors.

This affect clearly indicates the striving from weakness to superiority, and the attempt to retain one's position and evade a feeling of powerlessness and inferiority.

C. THE MISUSE OF EMOTION

No one understood the meaning and value of the affects and emotions until it was discovered that they were valuable instruments to overcome the feeling of inferiority, and to elevate the personality and obtain its recognition. The faculty of showing emotion has a wide application in the psychic life. Once a child has learned that he can tyrannize his environment by fury, or sadness, or weeping, arising out of a feeling of neglect, he will test this method of obtaining domination over his environment again and again. In this way he falls easily into a behavior pattern which allows him to react to insignificant stimuli with his typical emotional response. He uses his emotions whenever they suit his needs. Preoccupation with emotion is a bad habit which occasionally becomes pathological. When this has occurred in childhood we find an adult who is constantly misusing his emotions. We have the picture of an individual who uses anger, sorrow, and all other affects in a playful way, as though they were puppets. This valueless and often unpleasant characteristic serves to rob emotions of their true value. Play-acting with emotions becomes a habitual response whenever such an individual is denied anything or whenever the dominance of his personality is threatened. Sorrow may be expressed with such violent cries that it becomes unpleasant because it too closely resembles a raucous personal advertisement. We have seen people who give the impression that they are competing with themselves in the degree of sorrow they could show.

The same misuse can be made of the physical accompaniments of emotion. It is well known that there are people who allow their anger to react so strongly upon their digestive systems that they vomit when they are infuriated. This mechanism expresses their hostility all the more transparently. The emotion of sadness is similarly associated with refusal to eat so that the sorrowful individual actually loses weight and veritably illustrates "the picture of sadness."

These types of misuse cannot be a matter of indifference with us, because they touch the other fellow's social feeling. The moment a neighbor expresses his friendly feeling for the sufferer the violent affects we have described cease. There are, however, individuals who crave the expression of another's friendliness to such an extent that they wish never to cease with their sorrow because only in this state do they feel some tangible elevation of their personality sense as a result of the many indications of the friendship and sympathy of their neighbors.

Even though our sympathies are associated with them in various degrees, anger and sorrow are disjunctive emotions. They do not serve to really bring men closer. Actually they separate by injuring the social feeling. Sorrow, it is true, eventually effects a union, but this union does not occur normally, because *both* parties do not contribute. It effects a distortion of the social feeling in which, sooner or later, the other fellow has to contribute the greater share!

D. DISGUST

The affect of disgust is marked by a disjunctive element, even though this is not so well marked as in the other affects. Physically, disgust occurs when the stomach walls are stimulated in a certain fashion. There are, however, also tendencies and attempts to "vomit" matter out of the psychic life. It is here that the disjunctive factor of the affect becomes visible. The subsequent events reinforce us in our opinion. Disgust is a gesture of aversion. The grimaces accompanying it signify a contempt for the environment, and the solution of a problem, with a gesture of discard. This affect can easily be misused by being made an excuse for removing oneself from an unpleasant situation. It is easy to simulate nausea, and once it is present one must, of necessity, escape from the particular social gathering in which one finds oneself. No other affect can be produced artificially so easily as disgust. By means of a special training, anyone can develop the ability of easily producing nausea; in this way a harmless affect becomes a powerful weapon against society, or an unfailing excuse for withdrawing from it.

E. FEAR AND ANXIETY

Anxiety is one of the most significant phenomena in the life of man. This affect becomes complicated by the fact that it is not only a disjunctive emotion, but like sorrow, it is capable of effecting a one-sided bond for one's fellows. A child escapes one situation by his fear, but he runs to the protection of someone else. The mechanism of *anxiety* does not directly demonstrate any superiority—indeed it seems to illustrate a defeat. In anxiety one seeks to make oneself as small as possible, but it is at this point that the conjunctive side of this affect, which carries with it at the same time a thirst for superiority, becomes evident. The anxious individuals flee into the protection of another situation, and attempt to fortify themselves in this way until they feel themselves capable of meeting and triumphing over the danger to which they feel exposed.

In this affect we are dealing with a phenomenon which is organically very deeply rooted. It is a reflection of the primitive fear which seizes all living things. Mankind is especially subject to this fear because of his weakness and insecurity in nature. So inadequate is our knowledge of the difficulties of life that a child can never of himself reconcile himself with it. Others must contribute whatever he lacks. The child senses these difficulties at the moment in which he enters life, and the conditions of living begin to influence him. There is always a danger that he will fail, in striving to compensate for his insecurity, and develop a pessimistic philosophy as a result. His dominant character trait becomes, therefore, a certain thirst for the help and consideration of his environment. The farther he stands from the solution of his life's problems, the more developed is his cautiousness. Should such children ever be forced to make an advance, they carry the gestures and plans of their retreat with them. They are always prepared for retreat, and naturally their most common and obvious character trait is the affect of anxiety.

We see the beginnings of opposition in the manner in which this affect is expressed, as in mimicry, but this opposition does not proceed aggressively nor in a straight line. A particularly clear insight into the workings of the soul is sometimes vouchsafed us when pathological degenerations of this affect occur. In these cases we clearly sense how the anxious individual reaches out for a helping hand, and seeks to draw another toward him, and chain him to his side.

Further study of this phenomenon leads us to considerations which we have already discussed under the character trait of anxiety. In this case we are dealing with individuals who demand support from someone, who need someone paying attention to them at all times. As a matter of fact it amounts to nothing more than the institution of a master-slave relationship, as if someone else had to be present to aid and support the anxious one. Investigate this further and one finds many people who go through life demanding particular recognitions. They have so far lost their independence (as a result of their insufficient and incorrect contact with life) that they demand exceptional privileges, with extraordinary violence. No matter how much they seek out the company of others, they have little social feeling. But let them show anxiety and fright, and they can create their privileged position again. Anxiety helps them evade the demands of life, and enslave all those about them. Finally it worms itself into every relationship in their daily lives, and becomes their most important instrument to effect their domination.

II. The Conjunctive Affects

A. JOY

Joy is an affect which most clearly bridges the distance from man to man. Joy does not brook isolation. Expressions of happiness as evinced in the search for a companion, in the embrace, and the like, arise in human beings who want to play together, to join together, or enjoy something together. The attitude is a conjunctive one. It is, so to speak, the reaching out of a hand to a fellow-man. It is similar to the radiation of warmth from one person to another. All the elements of conjunction are present in this affect. To be sure, we are again dealing with human beings who are attempting to overcome a feeling of dissatisfaction, or of loneliness, so that they may attain a measure of superiority, along our frequently demonstrated line from below to above. Happiness, as a matter of fact, is probably the best expression for the conquest of difficulties. Laughter, with its liberating energy, its freedom-giving powers, goes hand in hand with happiness, and represents, so to speak, the keystone of this affect. It reaches out beyond the personality and entwines itself in the sympathies of others.

Even this laughter and this happiness may be misused for

personal ends. Thus a patient who was afraid to allow the feeling of insignificance to arise in him, showed signs of joy at the report of a deadly earthquake. When he was sad he felt powerless. He therefore fled from sadness and attempted to approach the opposite affect, joy. Another misuse of happiness is the expression of joy at the pain of others. A joy which arises at the wrong time or in the wrong place, which denies the social feeling and destroys it, is nothing but a disjunctive affect, an instrument of conquest.

B. SYMPATHY

Sympathy is the purest expression of the social feeling. Whenever we find sympathy in a human being we can in general be sure that his social feeling is mature, because this affect allows us to judge how far a human being is able to identify himself with his fellow men.

Perhaps more wide-spread than this affect itself, is its conventional misuse. This consists in posing as an individual who has a great deal of social feeling; the misuse inheres in its exaggeration. Thus there are individuals who crowd to the scene of a disaster in order to be mentioned in the newspapers, and achieve a cheap fame without actually doing anything to help the sufferers. Others seem to have a lust for tracking down another's misfortune. Professional sympathizers and alms-givers are not to be divorced from their activity for they are actually creating a feeling of their own superiority over the miserable and poverty-stricken victims whom they are alleged to be helping. That great knower of human beings, La Rochefoucauld, has said: "We are always prepared to find a measure of satisfaction in the misfortune of our friends."

A mistaken attempt has been made to connect our enjoyment of tragic dramas, to this phenomena. It has been said that the onlooker feels holier than the characters upon the stage. This does not fit the majority of people, for our interest in a tragedy arises for the most part in the desire for self-knowledge and self-instruction. We do not lose sight of the fact that it is only a play, and we make use of the action to give us an added impetus in our preparations for life.

C. MODESTY

Modesty is an affect which is conjunctive and disjunctive at one and the same time. This affect, too, is part of the structure of our social feeling, and as such is not to be separated from our psychic life. Human society were impossible without this affect. It occurs wherever it would seem that the value of one's personality was about to sink, or where one's conscious self-evaluation might be lost. This affect is strongly transferred to the body, the transference consisting in the expansion of the peripheral capillaries. A congestion in the skin capillaries, recognized as a blush, occurs. This occurs usually in the face, but there are some people who blush all over their body.

The external attitude is one of withdrawal. It is a gesture of isolation bound up with a slight depression which amounts to a readiness to desert from a threatening situation. Downcast eyes and coyness are movements of flight, showing definitely that modesty is a disjunctive affect.

Like other affects modesty may be misused. Some people blush so easily that all their relationships to their fellows are poisoned by this disjunctive trait. Its value as a mechanism of isolation becomes obvious when it is thus misused.

APPENDIX

CONCLUSION

We have attempted to show in this book that the soul arises from a hereditary substance which functions both physically and psychically. Its development is entirely conditioned by social influences. On the one hand the demands of the organism must find fulfillment, and on the other the demands of human society must be satisfied. In this context does the soul develop, and by these conditions is its growth indicated.

We have investigated this development further, have discussed the capabilities and faculties of perception, recollection, emotion, and thinking, and finally, we have considered traits of character and affects. We have shown that all these phenomena are connected by indivisible bonds; that on the one hand they are subject to the rule of communal life, and on the other they are influenced by individual striving for power and superiority, so that they express themselves in a specific, individual, and unique pattern. We have shown how the goal of superiority of the individual, modified by his social feeling, according to the degree of its development in any concrete case, gives rise to specific character traits. Such traits are in no way hereditary, but are developed in such a way that they fit into the mosaic pattern which arises from the origin and source of the psychic development, and lead in a unit direction to the goal which is constantly present, more or less consciously, for everyone.

A number of these character traits and affects which are valuable indicators for the understanding of a human being, have been discussed at some length, whereas others have been neglected. We have shown that a definite degree of ambition and vanity appears in every human being according to the individual striving for power. In this expression we can clearly discover his striving for power and its manner of activity. We have also shown how the exaggerated development of ambition and vanity prevent the orderly development of the individual. The development of the social feeling is thus either stunted or made quite impossible. Because of the disturbing influence of these two traits, the evolution of the social feeling is not only inhibited but the power-hungry individual is led to his own destruction.

This law of psychic development seems to us to be irrefutable. It is the most important indicator to any human being who wishes to build up his destiny consciously and openly, rather than to allow himself to be the victim of dark and mysterious tendencies. These researches are experiments in the science of human nature, a science which cannot otherwise be taught or cultivated. The understanding of human nature seems to us indispensable to every man, and the study of its science, the most important activity of the human mind.

Which of these popular new Permabooks do you want?

(Continued on next page)

New titles are added monthly. See your local
dealer for these and other new Permabooks.